KITCHENS, OR SINK

MATTHEW INGLE is Life President and founder of Howdens, the kitchen and joinery company he started in 1995. He left school at seventeen and went to work at a timber yard in Huddersfield, before joining Magnet kitchens. When he was made redundant from Magnet in 1994, he decided to start his own business; today, Howdens is listed on the FTSE 100. Matthew lives in Yorkshire with his wife and dogs.

KITCHENS, OR SINK

HOW HOWDENS SUCCEEDED
AGAINST ALL THE ODDS

Matthew Ingle

Illustrated by Jeff Kindleysides

HEAD
of ZEUS

An Apollo Book

The author royalties from this book will be donated
to the Howdens charitable foundation, the NSPCC,
the RNLI and the RSPCA.

First published in the UK in 2022 by Head of Zeus Ltd,
part of Bloomsbury Publishing Plc

9 7 5 3 1 2 4 6 8

A catalogue record for this book is available
from the British Library.

ISBN (HB): 9781803283685
ISBN (E): 9781803283661

Typeset by benstudios.co.uk

Printed and bound in Great Britain
by CPI Group (UK) Ltd, Croydon CR0 4YY

Head of Zeus Ltd
First Floor East
5–8 Hardwick Street
London EC1R 4RG

WWW.HEADOFZEUS.COM

For Sarah

CONTENTS

Preface

How Did We Get Here?

In 1971 I left school with four O Levels and went to work in a timber yard in Huddersfield.

I then joined a management training programme with Magnet, the kitchen and joinery company, which had been founded in Bingley in West Yorkshire by my great-grandfather Tom Duxbury in 1918 when – so the story goes – he exchanged his horse Magnet for a firelighting company.

I worked at Magnet's door factory in Grays in Essex and then at the Bingley depot, before becoming a buyer for the company, and then development director, and eventually a general manager, until in 1994 I was made redundant and found myself for the first time in my life without a job.

A year later, in 1995, I founded my own kitchen and joinery company, named Howdens, a public company which, at the time of writing, has a £2.1 billion turnover, employs more than 10,000 staff, has over 800 depots, operates two manufacturing plants in the UK, with profits in excess of £390 million per annum, and which has made a huge investment over the years in UK manufacturing, logistics and product design. Today, Howdens is worth more than both the Royal Mail and ITV.

This book is the story of how I went from a low point in my life – no job, no income, kicked out of the old family firm, with only an idea for a business with no name, no products, no buildings and no backers – to becoming the Chief Executive of a Royal Warrant-holding company listed on the FTSE 250. I think it's a story worth telling – not because it's about me, but because it tells us something about the past, present and future of manufacturing in the UK.

Howdens started trading in October 1995 – a little over a year after my unceremonious departure from Magnet. We opened with fourteen depots and twenty-eight staff. Our first week's turnover was the princely sum of £17,194. Ten of the original depots were within the M25, two on the south coast, and two in the west country. Our mission was simple: to supply the kitchen and joinery requirements of the small builder and contractor from local stock nationwide, assuring best local price and 'no callback' quality. Howdens is now the UK's leading trade supplier of kitchens, supplying more than a quarter of a million small businesses with over 4 million kitchen cabinets, 3 million doors, 1 million appliances and more than 400,000 complete kitchens every year.

How did we get here?

I am writing this book largely to answer that simple question – to get things clear in my own mind about the history of the business. I've certainly been extremely lucky, both in my professional and private life, but the success of a business like Howdens is not just down to luck – how could it be? Every year thousands of businesses are founded and thousands more fail. Only a few succeed, and only a very few on the scale that Howdens has succeeded. We clearly made some very good decisions, at the right time, in the right place, and with the right people. But looking back over the history of the business I've been struck by the many ironies and paradoxes that have characterised the story of our success: our triumphs were often built on setbacks and failures, with what at first appeared to be disasters turning into extraordinary opportunities.

So, the book is a reckoning not only with our success, but also with the many struggles that led to that success. It's not a straightforward rags-to-riches story. It's a true story about our long journey towards our goal.

It will become clear during the course of this book – if it's not clear already – that I am no business guru. There is nothing particularly special about me. I have no big ideas or grand theories. I did not excel at school. I did not go to university. I have little or no experience outside of my own narrow field of expertise, which is trade manufacturing and sales, in kitchens and joinery, largely based in the north of England, which remains a deeply unfashionable area of enterprise and endeavour in an often overlooked area of the UK. What I am is a businessman, pure and simple, Yorkshire born and bred, and proud to be so. And what I have tried to do here is exactly what I tried to do in business: to identify problems, to explore possibilities and offer solutions, and wherever I can to simplify the complex, to make things clear to myself and others. In business, as in life, there are no shortcuts to success, but I have included here some examples of those pithy little phrases that at Howdens became known as Ingleisms, the sayings and stories that I often used to sum up or illustrate a point – what I call home truths.

(If you *are* looking for a shortcut to success, I'm afraid the best I can offer is my own personal favourite Ingleism, Skipton Market Rules – see p. 79. If you follow Skipton Market Rules, whatever your business, you won't go far wrong.)

My vision for Howdens was jotted down on a single sheet of paper sometime after I was made redundant from Magnet and at some point before we got the business fully underway. I have that piece of paper still. It reads:

> Howdens solves problems for small builders doing joinery work. It is about fitting into their society and not letting them down, associating with those people who run their own business who don't get paid until a job is complete and satisfactory, which means that it looks good, meets standards, is easy to fit, doesn't break, is available locally and when required, and with parts that can be swapped. We offer credit terms, giving a good margin using a confidential discount, excluding retail, offering a nice trade environment, maintaining the same staff – always the same faces – with no room for fairy stories.

No room for fairy stories. That's perhaps the key: the reality of Howdens turned out to be a winning formula that everyone connected with the business could call their own, a philosophy and a business model that allowed us to grow and succeed beyond even my own early dreams and expectations.

In order to tell the story of Howdens I have had to tell a little of my own story – about my background and beliefs and ideas. But this is not really a book about me. My experiences are interesting – if at all – only because they are illustrative, because they relate to larger realities and principles. The story of Howdens is my story, but it's also a story that belongs to all the people who made the business. It's a book about the forebears and the founders of the businesses that came before Howdens – the Duxbury family on my mother's side, and the Ingle family on my father's. It's about the many great teachers who helped to guide my thinking and understanding – from my actual teachers at school to renowned figures in the world of business, people like David Barclay and David Ogilvy. It's also about the many unsung heroes, the virtuosos and the grafters, the masters of their craft, the people whose brilliance and expertise and sheer hard work have made our business what it is today. It's a book about a series of decisions, of moments of crisis and of learning, of validation and of triumph, shared by many people over many years.

I am not naive enough to think that these stories and lessons might be applicable in all circumstances in all businesses to all people, but nor am I arrogant enough to think that these victories have been ours and ours alone. Howdens is our story – but I very much hope that there might be something here for you, whoever you are, whatever has brought you to read this unlikely tale.

I know that there will be people reading this book who will have worked for Howdens, and who still work for Howdens, as well as our customers past and present. I owe you all a particular debt of gratitude. I set out to make Howdens like home, the sort of business our fathers and mothers might have been proud to been a part of. That was my aim and intention. And you made it a reality. It is my hope that our children and our children's children might be a part of Howdens too, and will feel the same way about it as we do – as good as it ever was, yesterday, today and forever.

Thank you.

So. This is a story about kitchens...

Storytelling:

Articulating the values of the brand...

'I set out to create a company our fathers would have been proud to use.'

...Two brothers working together...

...They make chicken sheds...

...They have a woodyard...

...They start to make Kitchens...

A community Set in 1930s Yorkshire

This is a story of Values...

...and start to grow their business.

The Pub Test

One of my chairmen at Howdens, Will Samuel, a man of extraordinarily broad business experience – banking, trade and
industry – always used to say that any business, no matter how
complex or grand, had to be able to stand up to the simple test
of a quick conversation down the pub.

Basically, when you meet someone in a pub or a bar – or in
any other social situation where you're brought together for
a few moments, a train journey, say, or when you're standing
at the school gates, or you're out on a walk somewhere – and
you're asked about your business, can you explain what it
is and how it's doing, in about thirty seconds, among all the
other distractions and hubbub and noise, and before they lose
interest and you lose interest and you both move on and start
talking about other more important things, like life, politics,
weather, or what's on the telly or the sport.

Can you explain your business to them? Yes or no? Brief,
honest, and to the point?

I have done my best in these chapters to bear in mind Will
Samuel's pub test. I've tried to answer the kind of questions
people have often asked me about our business in casual
conversation, in pubs, in bars, on trains, as well as in big
presentations to the City and to shareholders, and to answer
those questions as clearly and as simply as I possibly can.

Who *are* you?

What *is* Howdens?

What do you do?

Where did the idea come from?

How did you get started?

Who was involved?

What were some of the highs?

What were some of the lows?

What's special about the way you do things?

Why should I care?

And if all this is true and yours was such a great business, and things were going so well, why on earth did you retire when you did?

How did it start, Matthew? And how will it all end?

I'll be brief, I'll be honest. And – as much as I can – to the point.

The Kangaroo Tail

I was born in Bradford in 1954. According to the Chinese calendar, 1954 was the year of the horse. Apparently, people who are born under the sign of the horse are hard-working, intelligent, cheerful, friendly and occasionally impatient. That sounds about right.

I was a pretty unremarkable child. I wasn't particularly bookish. I wasn't particularly good at sport. But from an early age I knew my own mind.

One of my earliest memories is from when I was at nursery school.

I must have been about four years old. I'd seen something on TV and I found a piece of string and I tied it to the back of my shorts and went to school: my kangaroo tail.

It went down a storm – everyone in my class wanted one.

So I was called to the front of the class. Our teacher was an old-school disciplinarian. There was a boy who used to mess around – the teacher used to tie his hands behind his back with baler twine.

I remember I was standing there with my piece of string tied to the back of my shorts and the teacher asked me what it was and I said it was my kangaroo tail and she said, Matthew, I'm sure a lot of your friends would like a kangaroo tail, let's share it out, shall we? And she took a big pair of scissors and she chopped that string into all these tiny little pieces. So everyone had a tiny piece of string – and no one had a kangaroo tail.

I don't know if I realised it then, but it was an important lesson: if you're not careful, your good ideas can easily be ruined by other people. Everyone is always going to want you to do things their way. Authority will always try and mess things up.

So – hold on to your kangaroo tail.

'Good Ideas Can be ruined by other people'

Shall I Wop Rop?

Tommy Thompson was the headmaster at my prep school. He was like something out of an old film. Black gown, black mortar board – the full works. It perhaps goes without saying that he was another strict disciplinarian. He'd beat you as soon as look at you, Tommy. There was an alleged incident, someone had done something or other – some misdemeanour or minor infraction of the rules – and no one would own up to it. If no one owns up, said Tommy, I shall have no choice but to beat every boy in the school. And when no one owned up, he duly did. He was as good as his word. It took him three whole days to work his way through the school. Dickensian is one way of describing it.

I can remember when I first arrived at school, we were at lunch in the big dining hall and I was chatting excitedly to a new friend of mine, a boy called Mark Ropner – I still know him now, Mark – and the place suddenly fell silent and Tommy Thompson roared, Bring him forwards, and so poor old Mark was hauled up in front of him and Mark was absolutely terrified, of course. What's your name, boy, asks Tommy. Rop... Ropner, sir, whimpers Mark. Well, boys, says Tommy, playing to the crowd, the question is, shall I wop Rop? Eh? Shall I wop Rop? Meaning: shall I beat him? Total silence in the dining hall. Put your hand up if you think I should. And everyone put their hand up. And now put your hand up if you think I should not. And I put my hand up. I didn't know any better – but I knew it was unfair.

Thank goodness, Tommy seemed surprised that someone was prepared to stand up to him. He looked around and he said, I think I'll take the advice of the young man at the back. And Mark Ropner was released. Tommy T did not wop Rop.

Sometimes, if you stand up to authority, if you stick to your principles and you do what's right, you won't get a beating. And even if you do, you'll have still done the right thing.

There was another time, we were in this old tower in the school and we were mucking around with a trap door that looked down on a classroom below – and the whole thing fell through. The trap door crashed down onto the floor below. It was a hell of a mess. And of course we scarpered and none of us said anything. But then we had to go to chapel twice a day and Tommy Thompson was standing there on the way out, shaking hands with every boy, and I thought, well, this is my chance to own up and tell him about the trap door. And so I did. I thought it was the right thing to do. I wanted to let you

Wop Rop

Stand up to authority – speak up – stand your ground.

know, sir, I said, I had a bit of an accident with the trap door in the tower and it caused a bit of a mess. Thanks for letting me know, Ingle, he said. And no more was said about it. We understood each other.

Now, to be clear: he was a terrifying man, Tommy Thompson. He wasn't exactly Wackford Squeers, but he wasn't far off. And those old English prep schools, there was a hell of a lot wrong with them. So I wouldn't say they didn't do any of us any harm – but they certainly taught me to speak up and stand my ground.

Shall I wop Rop? No, sir.

The Guinea Pig

I remember when I was a child I really, really wanted a guinea pig – and I wasn't allowed one. No way, said my mother. You're not having a guinea pig.

And then one day, for some reason, I was with my mother in the car, and we were travelling from Leeds, and we stopped in Malton to do some shopping. It's a lovely little market town, Malton. All sorts of shops. I was about nine or ten years old. And I was left in the car, and with my mother off getting the shopping I saw my opportunity.

I got out of the car, found myself a pet shop and bought myself a guinea pig, with my pocket money, just like that. Job done. The pet shop owner put him in a little brown cardboard box for me – I can see it now. And I went back to the car and waited for my mother.

Mother returned and we set off and eventually she said

what's that scratching noise, Matthew? And I told her it was a guinea pig. But I said you couldn't have a guinea pig, she said. It's too late now, I said.

When we got home I remember my father built a little hutch and then my grandfather sent me a book on guinea pig care. It all worked out. It was fine.

Sometimes if you want things done, you do have to take action. Someone needs to decide and get on with things, which allows other people to get on with things. In my career in business I have met a lot of people who are lot smarter than me. I have met a lot of people who are better educated than me, who have better ideas, and bigger plans. But I think if I have a skill, it's making decisions, and allowing other people to do the same.

Can we do it? Yes we can? Right, then off we go.

Let's buy a guinea pig.

The Final Over

My mother Betty Duxbury was an extraordinary woman. Strong-minded, wilful, determined – are some of the words that might apply. There are others.

She loved horse racing, Mother. She also enjoyed cricket. She used to play at school. She wasn't a bad player. And of all the things she ever said there's one in particular that I remember. Matthew, she said, if you're the captain and it's the closing over and all the other team need is three runs to win, you don't give the ball to your bowler, you take the ball and you bowl yourself. You take responsibility. You don't let anyone else take the blame. You are the captain. You sort it out. Play up, play the game.

It's a good lesson – and one I took to heart.

When mother died a few years ago there was a bit of bother with the will. I spoke to my lawyer and she said, Matthew, there's a bit of a problem. So we met for lunch. Well, this is a bit awkward, she said. Your mother has left you some money. Fine, I said. I'm an only child. I couldn't see it being that complicated. But there's a condition, she said. What's the condition? I'm afraid, Matthew, your mother has specified that in order for you to inherit, you have to change your name.

My mother's maiden name was Duxbury – she became Ingle when she married my father. I would only inherit if I took her maiden name. I would have to become Matthew Duxbury.

My lawyer, being a lawyer, suggested that this was a simple matter: all I had to do was change my name, inherit the money, and then I could always change it back again.

But to me it was a matter of principle. My name is Matthew Ingle. It is not Matthew Duxbury. My parents' divorce – in my teens – had been a very unhappy affair and my mother had behaved rather badly. What happens if I refuse? I asked my lawyer. Well – if you refuse, Matthew, your mother has specified that for twenty-one years we have to sponsor a race at Ascot or at York in the Duxbury name and that after twenty-one years what little money remains will go to charity.

She had really thought it through.

Now, I happen to think that the charity is a very worthy cause. So I could have let it go – I could simply have refused to change my name, and my mother's money would have been wasted at the races, until the charity ended up with a few measly pounds at the end of it all. I could have let my mother have her way.

But like I say, it was a matter of principle. So after I spoke to my lawyer, I spoke to my mother's lawyer. There's absolutely nothing we can do about it, Matthew, she said. But I don't think it's fair, I said. It doesn't matter what you think, she said. It's the law. In which case I don't think the law is fair, I said. Her money was left in trust to her when she was Betty Ingle, not Betty Duxbury, so it seems not merely unreasonable but unjust. It doesn't matter whether you think it's unreasonable or unjust, she said. Yes, it does, I said. You do know what kind of person I am, I said? Yes, she said.

I will find a solution, I said.

And I did.

I called another lawyer, a man named Andrew O'Keeffe – appropriately known in the business as A OK. I explained the situation to A OK and he thought about it and suggested that we contact the charity, who would be the final beneficiaries of my mother's will, and make them an offer of some money now rather than in twenty-one years' time, and see what they said. It turned out that the charity were very happy with that arrangement and agreed to forego their rights as the ultimate beneficiaries.

So, I got to inherit, did not have to change my name – and what seemed like an intractable problem was in fact something that was relatively easily resolved.

In death, as in life, my mother set a number of challenges for me, which I have done my best to overcome. She insisted on being buried in a churchyard that had been closed since 1986, for example – but again, we sorted it out. And in the end, everyone was a winner. Nobody came off worse. Though my mother may not have seen it that way.

On her gravestone I had engraved the words of one of my favourite songs by Leonard Cohen.

Play up, play the game – all the way to the final over.

Motherhood

All of the business books I've ever read – and I try to avoid them, to be absolutely honest – always seem to imply that business is really a man's game. It's all about everyone jostling for position; people are in it for themselves and damn the consequences. Business is portrayed as real macho man stuff. And sometimes it is. You do have to be pretty tough, you do have to make difficult and unpleasant decisions, and you do have to be able to withstand a lot of criticism and a lot of flak – and I've known plenty of women in my personal and professional life who are more than capable of doing exactly that.

So, yes, business is macho man stuff – for both men *and* women.

It's also a bit like motherhood.

In business, like a mother, you just have to be there. You have to be seen. You have to be prepared to do what's necessary. You have to allow people to talk, you have to allow problems to surface. And then you need to act. It doesn't mean you've got all the answers. If you've got a sick child, does the mother have the solution to a broken leg or a toothache? No, of course not. She may not be able to fix it, but she doesn't pretend it's not a problem. If she has a child with a broken leg she doesn't pretend it's a tummy ache and it's going to go away all by itself. She realises that she's going to have to get her child to the hospital, and she's going to stay with them until it's fixed. A mother doesn't deny a problem – she says fine, let's get this sorted.

And not only that – it's usually the case that a mother isn't dealing with just a single problem. It's usually the case that a mother has dozens of problems she's having to address at the same time. It's a never-ending problem-raising and problem-solving job, motherhood – that's just what it is.

Similarly, business demands bravery, it demands patience, it requires people being prepared to face facts and figure things out from first principles. You can call it what you like. Leadership, guidance, taking care and responsibility of things – motherhood.

D-Day

My father, Douglas Baines Ingle, was a great influence on me. In many ways, I owe him my success.

He was a tanner from Leeds. He'd gone to Leeds University, joined the family business, and then when the war came he volunteered. The story goes that he was driving his beloved Norton motorbike to join his ship up in Glasgow but only got as far as Settle and couldn't get the bike up the hill. So he took the train instead, left the Norton behind, and lo and behold, when he eventually returned to Settle the bike was still there.

He was in Combined Operations, my father – combined navy and army. Their general purpose was to harass the Nazis by land, sea and air, and in particular via amphibious raids.

He ended up as first officer on LCT 455 – one of those long, low-slung boats you often see in the old films, top speed ten knots, with a tiny little wheelhouse – and on D-Day, 6 June 1944, they were part of the initial assault, Operation Overlord. Their job was to land at the easternmost landing site of the invasion, Sword Beach, between Ouistreham and Saint-Aubin-sur-Mer. They had the 13th/18th Royal Hussars on board, Queen Mary's Own, who were in these little floating tanks, the famous Sherman DDs (Donald Ducks), and their instructions were to drop them 8,000 yards out at sea, which is a long way out. They'd obviously got to know the men in the tanks on the way over and the skipper on LCT 455 was an old Grimsby trawler man who said there was no way they were going to drop their lads that far out in the water, they were going to take them right up onto the beach. Which they did – which was a pretty dangerous manoeuvre, the trouble with a tank landing craft being that you can certainly land it on a beach, but you're going to have a hell of a lot of trouble getting it back off. Anyway, somehow, thank goodness, they made it. I have a letter from the flotilla officer to my father, dated 10 August 1944, which reads, 'So you can be happy that you enabled a very valuable contribution to the assault to take place with almost parade ground precision and all your tremendous efforts and work was more than repaid.'

When he came home from the war he went back into the family business and caught anthrax from the hides brought in from Africa and was scarred for rest of his life, on his face. The family business eventually wound up and my father retired early to live on the Isle of Man, where he lived to a ripe old age. He had a fine mind, was super-fit, and he died on 10 December 2008. So he never got to see the great success of Howdens, but he did see the beginnings – and, as it happens, because he died when he did I inherited some money, which meant I could buy shares in the business, meaning that I could back myself and the business when no one else was interested.

I didn't get to see him before he died, but my father got me safely landed.

Gold Stars

At school I was always – and I mean *always* – at the bottom of the class. I worked hard, but I just never seemed to get on. I was sent to hearing specialists, psychologists, psychiatrists – you name them, I was sent to them. The question was always, what's wrong with Matthew? And they couldn't find anything wrong with me. Because there was nothing wrong with me. As it happens, I was dyslexic – still am. Dyslexia. Dyspraxia. You name it. I can barely ride a bike, and it takes me a while to read a book. But dyslexia/dyspraxia/dyswhatever wasn't a diagnosis back then. You were just stupid. Really, I was just different.

I think those early school experiences had a big impact on me. To this day I don't have a lot of time for people who like to make others look or feel stupid. I don't like people who try and hold others back. I don't like people who encourage you to feel like a victim. And I'm not interested in status or rank, high or low. I know that everyone wants to feel valued. Everyone wants a gold star – even those at the bottom of the class.

In business, this tends to make me sympathetic towards those who had bad luck at school but who later in life decide to build a career. They're exactly the sort of people we employ at Howdens. I've always liked people who work hard, who set out to create things and make things happen. I tend to dislike all those layers of middle management that you get in business, and all those people who focus on problems rather than solutions, people who moan and criticise and blame. I like the doers: the people who actually do stuff. I think they deserve the praise. They deserve the acknowledgement. They deserve the stars.

Walking the Dogs

So I did not excel at school – except when it came to looking after the dogs. Tommy Thompson, to grant him his due, realised that I may not have made much of an academic, but that I might be able to make myself useful at something. He put me in charge of looking after his dogs. Struggling with the day's lessons, Matthew? Well, we'll get you out to walk the dogs. Not much good at games, Matthew? We'll get you out and walk the dogs. I remember he had a labrador and an English setter, and the English setter was a pretty powerful beast, far too big and strong for a young lad like me to manage. So I had to wear this belt, with the dog tied to the belt, and if it got too out of hand all you could do was throw yourself on the ground. That'd put a stop to it.

Honestly, the best thing that happened to me at school was looking after those dogs. We had all sorts of adventures. They gave me a great sense of pride and responsibility. They taught me how to cope with all sorts of situations. The school was near Catterick Garrison and I remember once I was out with the dogs and an army truck turned over and I ran all the way back to school with the dogs and alerted the teacher to it – and two days later, two huge bars of chocolate turned up, as a thank you from the barracks. They kept me company, the dogs, and gave me courage.

I've kept dogs ever since. My family have always kept dogs. I remember my grandfather had a chocolate poodle named MU, given to him by the Mothers' Union, and a white miniature poodle named Pudsey, which he'd got from Pudsey – and as a child I'd take them for a walk using an old washing line. We have cocker spaniels now – dutiful, intelligent, friendly, an excellent working dog, the cocker spaniel. My first dog back in 1981 was a cocker spaniel called Fly. Wonderful dog. It would sit behind the seat in the car. You could take it anywhere. A dog will let you fly.

Dogs are calming. They give purpose to a walk. They add to the domestic routine. I just think it's good to have a dog around the place. They're sensitive beings – and they keep you in touch with what's real and what matters. Indeed, if I had to attribute my success to just three things I'd say my wife, Yorkshire, and the dogs. Though not necessarily in that order.

Le Rosey

After prep school I was sent to school in Switzerland. Not that I had any choice in the matter. I was just a child. I remember I was given a ticket and put on a plane at Leeds Bradford, aged twelve, and then I had to change at Heathrow and duly arrived in Geneva with a few francs in my pocket to get myself to school. It was a great experience, the journey there. I had to learn pretty quickly. Simple stuff, like being clear about where I was going. I was in a foreign country, I didn't have the language. It doesn't matter how clever you are in those circumstances, you're entirely dependent on other people. You have to learn to trust people, and hope that they might point you in the right direction. It gives you confidence. It makes you independent.

As for my actual education, well you can imagine: if you're dyslexic in English and you're trying to learn French and Italian... It was an absolute disaster. I probably learnt more up in the mountains skiing than I did in the classroom.

But I enjoyed the school. It was a place called Le Rosey, in Rolle, on the shores of Lake Geneva, between Nyon and Lausanne. It's a beautiful setting, in this old chateau, fully equipped in every way, and I was there among the children of the rich and famous – the big shipping families and banking families, the sons and daughters of magnates and moguls and tycoons, kings and queens. It was really quite a place, and quite a cast of characters. The teachers were extraordinary.

But the school nurse was something else.

She was called Mademoiselle Keller. The classic nurse uniform, plus these big dark glasses with orange-tinted lenses, and she wore these white high heels and she would clack down the corridor... She was absolutely terrifying. She ran a sort of makeshift surgery every day in this little room with a couple of shelves of medicine and a couch. There was always a queue outside the door, and people wandering in and out. She basically had four cures for everything. If you had a cold or the flu she made you gargle with salt water, dosed you up with some syrup, and would then take a large pipette and squirt some nasty thick brown liquid down each nostril. You certainly didn't want that stuff down your shirt. If you had an upset tummy she gave you a tumblerful of Pernod – which certainly does the trick. And if you were really sick she'd make you lie down on the couch and pull your trousers down, and then she'd insert a large vet's thermometer up your nether-end, with an old horse blanket thrown over you to protect your dignity. That soon sorted you out. Anything worse, she'd call a doctor. I wasn't sick very often.

As for the pupils – alumni of Le Rosey, *les anciens Roséen*, include the Shah of Iran, Prince Rainier, the Duke of Kent, King Fuad II of Egypt, King Juan Carlos of Spain, the Aga Khan, along with various Metternichs, Al-Fayeds, Niarchos, Rockefellers, Rothschilds and so on and so forth. Some of the kids there got away with absolute murder. There was one lad who had all these ultraviolet lights set up in his room – for which purposes you can imagine – and another whose room was blacked out entirely, goodness only knows why. It was a place of extraordinary privilege. Looking back now, the mind boggles. I don't know what my parents were thinking.

It's not that there weren't rules. On the contrary, the headmaster during my time there was the legendary Colonel Louis Johannot, who was one of the highest-ranking officers in the Swiss Army. He was a huge man, Joe, and with all sorts of interesting ideas. You weren't allowed to drink at the school, for example, unless you were drinking with him, in which case it was fine. And we were taught how to hunt and shoot – useful life skills. I remember once my father wrote to Joe. He wasn't happy with my academic performance. And Joe wrote back – you have nothing to worry about, Mr Ingle. Matthew's a perfectly good student. He arrives on time, he gets on with people. And these are the things that really matter. One hour before midnight is worth two after, Joe would always say. He had all these little mantras. And as I went through my business career I realised he was right. Be on time. Turn up. Be pleasant. Simple, basic stuff.

I learnt a lot in Switzerland – and then completed my education in Huddersfield.

The Timber Yard

I left Rosey in 1971 with my four O Levels and returned to England.

I had no real idea what I might do with myself, but my mother was a Duxbury. The Duxbury family owned Magnet Joinery, and my uncle Tom Duxbury agreed they'd take me on. You can join the business, Matthew, said Uncle Tom, but first you have to go and work in a timber yard for a couple of years. It was a tradition back then, in Yorkshire. If you were going into a family business, you'd spend some time outside the business, getting to know the trade. Which is how I ended up at Jarratt, Pyrah and Armitage of Huddersfield. Timber Merchants, Dealers in Mahogany, Wainscot and Fancy Woods, All Descriptions of Wood Turnings and Moulds Kept In Stock Or Made To Order. Softwood. Hardwood. Plywood. Wallboard. Dry Yellow Pine.

I may have been educated – at considerable expense – at Le Rosey in Switzerland, but my finishing school was Jarratt, Pyrah and Armitage of Huddersfield.

It was on Quay Street, JPA, right by the old turnbridge on the canal, just off Watergate and the Old Leeds Road. As soon as I arrived, I realised that this was another world. I'd come from a place where I'd been rubbing shoulders with the sons and daughters of the rich and famous. JPA was the opposite. There was nothing glamorous about Quay Street. I absolutely loved it.

Johnny Jagger was the foreman of the yard. He was about five foot tall, Johnny, plain-speaking, no-nonsense, a leather apron with his job sheets tucked in the pouch at the front. This was 1971: the canal boats had only just stopped coming in to load and unload. Everyone in the yard still had the old timber jackets with big shoulder pads for carrying logs. It was like something out of the nineteenth century. We still had an old steam engine driving all the machines – a big old engine. I remember a bloke called Matt was the engine stoker – the boiler was underground – and he had to stay there underground all day, Matt, to keep the steam engine going, and if you asked nicely he'd let you warm up your pies by the boiler.

JPA taught me how to deal with the Great British Public – you'd be serving everyone from a little old lady coming in for a piece of wood to fix a panel in her door, to builders in a screaming hurry, to wheeler-dealer contractors doing complete fit-outs. I certainly had a lot to learn. I had to learn that wood isn't just brown, for example, and that you get all sorts of wood – hardwood, softwood, redwood, whitewood, pine, fir, larch, spruce, teak, and so on. I had to learn to distinguish my baluster from my balustrade, a bead from a bevel and my mullions from my muntins, my panel products from my particleboard. JPA gave me a brilliant grounding in the world of timber; really I've worked in timber ever since. When I was running Howdens, people didn't always expect me to know too much about our actual products. JPA ensured I knew everything I needed to know, and more.

The lads working in the timber yards back then were no-nonsense individuals. And they were absolutely huge – and I mean like giants. Back then, working in the timber yards, you had to be built like a circus strongman. And everyone had missing fingers, of course – there were a hell of a lot of missing fingers in the timber yards in those days.

Anyway, I remember there was one bloke who was a bit of a ruffian – big scar across his face, massive. A pretty nasty piece of work. There was no drinking at lunchtime when you were working in the timber yard: there were saws everywhere, machinery. You wouldn't want to be mucking around with them if you'd had a couple of pints at lunch. So you had a ten-minute break in the morning, then half an hour at lunch, just enough time to eat your sandwich or your pie, and then ten minutes at three o'clock, and all finished by five. And one day we'd finished our lunch and I was standing in the yard and along comes the big scarface fella, swaying from side to side. He'd had a few, to say the least. And I remember as clear as if it were yesterday, Johnny Jagger saying to me, right lad, get

Characters - it takes all sorts.

SCARFACE

yourself a bearer – which is a piece of wood, 3" by 2" – and get ready, just in case. He can be a handful when he's been drinking. And sure enough, Scarface comes up and he stands in front of us and it all starts kicking off and Johnny has his own little bearer and when things start to get really nasty, Johnny just takes his bearer and knocks him out, knocks him out cold. Right lad, he says to me. Go and get the sideloader and put this fella down the end of the yard on a pallet. Which is what we did.

I couldn't believe that they'd keep him on after all that. But it didn't bother Johnny Jagger in the slightest. He was a good worker when he wasn't drinking, Scarface.

Johnny and all the lads at JPA taught me a hell of a lot – not least that if there's a problem, grab yourself a bearer, find a quick solution and move on.

Flat-Pack Coffins

In the old days, if you were an apprentice in the timber yards you were often sent off on some fool's errand. A long weight. A glass hammer. A bucket of steam. Elbow grease. A bender straightener. A fresh new bubble for the spirit level. All of that sort of thing. You were treated like people used to be treated in the workplace. It was all good fun. You took it in good part. I'm sure the same things happen today, though on the quiet: pranks, jokes, initiations.

So one day, this bloke comes into the yard and he says, I've been sent to see you. Right, I say. I've come for a flat-pack coffin, he says. Aye, right, I say. I think it's a wind-up. I don't know who you are, I say, but I'm not going to get you a flat-pack coffin, and you can tell whoever sent you that I'm not going to get you one. No, no, says this fellow. Seriously, he says, I'm here for a flat-pack coffin. Do you think I was born yesterday? I say. And there's a bit of back and forth until I realise this bloke is deadly serious. He's not mucking about. He really has come for a coffin. A flat-pack coffin.

I think they're on the third floor of the old mill, he says. All right, I say. But I'm still a bit sceptical. You go up the steps ahead of me and I'll follow right behind, I say. And we clamber up this old ladder and into one of the old storage rooms and sure enough, in this filthy old room there's a pile of flat-pack coffins. I can't believe it. Flat-pack coffins. Why do you need a flat-pack coffin, I ask. He says, why do you think? I'm an undertaker, and it's an orphanage job, and they haven't got any money, so a flat-pack's the best I can do.

Now, it's a silly story, really – a true story, but a silly story. But it taught me another important lesson. Just because I think this or that, that's not the point. You want a flat-pack coffin? Really? No problem, sir. Your job is to give your customer what they need. You're there to fix their problems – not to cause them more.

3' 2" ¹/₈ – Exactly

There's a wise old carpenter's saying – measure twice, cut once. Good advice.

I'd been at Jarratt, Pyrah and Armitage for about six months and a builder came in for some wainscoting. I'd got a bit of a reputation for reliability by this time. I was fastidious. I was always keen to get it right, to do it properly. Anyway, I'd dealt with this particular bloke before and someone else was going to serve him but he said, no, I want the posh lad to do it – meaning me. He wanted the wainscoting cut to 3' 2" ¹/₈ – exactly. Not roughly, exactly. 3' 2" ¹/₈ . There was no one else who'd be willing to do it. He wanted someone who was prepared to cut it to his precise specification so that there'd be no waste and he could put it straight on the walls. You're either prepared to do what's required, to enable someone to get their job done – or you're not. It doesn't matter who you are. Builders are busy people. It's not just about price, it's about the service. Can you help me with exactly what I need. No? Fine, well, move over, we'll have to get the posh lad to do it.

Another time, I remember it was snowing. It was the middle of winter. I was working in the hardwood department and a builder came in, looking for a staircase. Now, a staircase might look straightforward to you but it's really an incredibly complex bit of engineering. You've got the stringers, the outer string and the inner string, which is the part of the stair attached to the wall; you've got the tread, the riser, the newel post, the spindle, the handrail, the nosing. It's a hell of a lot of timber, a staircase – precision-cut timber. And anyway, this builder comes in looking for a staircase, and I'm looking outside at the weather and the last thing I want to do is go and get a staircase out for him. So I say, if you just let me know what you want, sir, I'll make a note and the office will let you know when we've got it out. No, no, lad, he says. I want it today. Right, I say. And when you say today, you mean you want it right now? That's right, lad, he says, right now.

So there's me, desperately looking around the yard for my

workmates, but they've all mysteriously disappeared inside into the warm and I'm on my own in the freezing cold with this bloke who wants a complete staircase, and I'm thinking about all the wood that's required. You'd usually do it in pine, a staircase. So I ask what kind of wood he's thinking about – and he says he wants it in mahogany. Mahogany. Right. Mahogany is a very tough wood, and it's a heavy wood – and all the mahogany we had was in logs and needed to be cut through on the lathes. This is turning into a very serious job. Are you looking for South American or African, I ask. African, he says. It's easier to find straight planks – and cheaper. I'll see if I can get someone to get the log down, I say, and then we can have a look at it. I manage to find this bloke called Stanley to give me a hand, and he helps me get the log down, but then he's off out of the cold and I'm left again with the builder so I say, have you got your drawings, and he has, and so I take the drawings and I look at this big mahogany log and I start to mark it out in thick crayon. I suppose you want it sawed up now, I say? If you wouldn't mind, lad. So I get the saw going, and we get it chopped up – and it's a full morning's work. It takes hours. And eventually off he goes.

A week later the yard manager comes down to see me. Ingle, he says, I don't know what you've done, but there's been a bloke in with a case of beer for you.

It was the builder who'd been in for the staircase. He wanted to say thank you. It was unbelievable.

In business, people want things done, and they want it done right. If you do it right, they might thank you. If you don't, they definitely won't.

Old Bill's Hut

When I was at the timber yard they were pulling down a lot of the old mills in Huddersfield. There was a lot of demolition going on – which meant there were always these rats thundering down the yard, fleeing the old buildings.

The timber yard was right on the Huddersfield Narrow Canal – and right next to the canal, twenty yards away from the main yard, was the old tanalising plant. It's a dirty old process, tanalising – you basically put your wood in a preservative, in these big tanks, under pressure. It's designed to protect the wood against decay. Copper chrome arsenic, we used. You wouldn't want to get that stuff on your hands – or anywhere else. You're not allowed to use it these days.

A bloke that everyone called Old Bill ran the tanalising plant. He'd been in Egypt during the war, Bill. He had this little shed, with an old armchair. And everything inside was covered in slime from the plant, including his overalls – and the armchair. But he was all right, Old Bill, and we'd often go over to the shed to keep him company or have lunch. Plug – the apprentice – would be sent off to go and get the sandwiches from a corner shop on the canal, where this big cat sat on the counter, next to the butter, which had an Anglepoise lamp above it, to keep it spreadable. And sometimes we'd also get soup, which we'd send down to Matt the stoker, to keep it warm. So we'd sit in Old Bill's shed on these little benches and have our lunch and on special occasions Bill might run a Super-8 blue movie, which was what you used to do for entertainment in the yards back then. It was an all-male working environment. It's just what it was like.

Anyway, one day Bill says, Look, lads, I need your help. I've got a rat and I'll tell you what we're going to do. We're going to leave some sandwiches out and the rat'll come. And we'll wait outside with some bearers and we'll send Plug round the back of the shed and when we hear the rat inside, Plug'll bang on the back of the shed, we'll open the door at the front, and we'll be ready for the little bastard.

Well, we put down the sandwiches and we waited for the rat and sure enough he shows up and Plug beats on the back of the shed and we open the door – and this rat came out of there liked greased lightning and he was straight into the canal and away. We didn't even come close to catching it.

But I tell you what I learnt from Old Bill – if you want to get something done, at the very least you need a plan, and you need a team of people. That was a simple lesson, a life lesson – one of many – from Old Bill's hut.

The rat in the cabin.

Duxburys

I was in the timber yard for two good years. I grew up in the timber yard. And then I joined the family business – Magnet. That was me launched upon my career – for which I have to thank the Duxbury family.

As it happens, both sides of my family were in manufacturing in West Yorkshire. On my mother's side there were the Duxburys, descendants of the original Tom Duxbury from Bingley, of great fame, who had founded Magnet when he swapped his horse for a firelighter business. And on my father's side were the lesser-known Ingles, the tanners, W. L. Ingle. If things had worked out differently I might now be working in leather. As it was, I went into Magnet – and I am forever glad that I did. Without Magnet, there would be no Howdens. Indeed, in many ways, in my opinion, Howdens as it is today is the continuation of the Duxbury family business – a tradition of joinery and manufacturing that goes back over 100 years.

Tom Duxbury was from a family of greengrocers. He was clearly a risk-taker. In August 1899 the *York Herald* announced an award for gallantry by the Royal Humane Society to 'Tom Duxbury, Greengrocer, Bingley, for plunging into the Leeds Liverpool Canal at Bingley on July 3rd and saving a man who had got into deep water while bathing.' A few years later he started the Magnet Firelighter Company at 6 Whitley Street, Bingley and in 1919 he set up another company, the Magnet Timber and Hardware Company, which bought and sold government surplus. He was a go-ahead sort of guy. He didn't rest on his laurels or let the grass grow under his feet. In 1922 advertisements in the *Yorkshire Post* and the *Leeds Intelligencer* read 'Government Surplus – Timbers, spars, posts, rails, tools for all trades, wire netting, corrugated sheets, roofing felt, ladders, barrows, paint, creosote oil: new American lawn mowers, 8" to 10" blades 37/6d. MAGNET, Bingley.'

This is not perhaps the time and place to tell the whole story of Magnet – that's another book. And it's not entirely my story to tell. But suffice it to say, many of the hard-won lessons learnt by the Duxburys over generations with Magnet were lessons that I did my best to put into practice with Howdens: innovate, adapt, give customers what they need rather than what you think they want, and always build on the best of what's gone before. There were also plenty of practices – both business and personal – from the Duxburys that I chose not to emulate. But again, that's for another time.

Anyway, the original Tom Duxbury was clearly an innovator, a true entrepreneur who saw a great opportunity after the First World War, buying cheap surplus stock from the government and converting old ammunition boxes into hen houses and furniture, eventually pioneering the mass production of joinery in the 1920s. In the years that followed, Magnet gradually expanded their product range even further, selling doors and windows and eventually producing joinery and components for the large construction companies. In 1936 Magnet was listed on the stock exchange, with the Duxbury family continuing to run the business. Which is where John – affectionately known as 'Mad Jack' – Duxbury comes in, my mother's father, my grandfather, son of the original Tom. It was Mad Jack who really got Magnet going. He put a rocket under the business, Jack Duxbury.

Mad Jack is the beginning of my own personal story with Magnet.

If Walls Could Talk

Once he got a hold of the reins of Magnet, Mad Jack did not hold back. He took on the unions, he took the business to America – and he built a big factory down in Grays in Essex. He was an absolute dynamo, Jack. He died in his early fifties but he was still around when I was a child: he was my direct connection to the family business, to Magnet. He was also my induction into the Duxbury's family ways.

What I remember most clearly about him is that he had this massive scar on his head. I can remember looking at it as a child. I don't know where he got it from – but wherever and however, he certainly looked like a man you wouldn't mess with. He was a front-row kind of guy, Jack Duxbury. The sort of person who'd refuse an injection at the dentist: a seriously hard man. (The story goes that he would indeed refuse an injection at the dentist. I can believe it.)

But he also had a kind of roguish charm about him. Even as a child I remember there was always stuff happening around him – there were dogs and animals and he smoked big cigars and he drank like a fish. There are all sorts of family stories about Mad Jack Duxbury – some of them repeatable. We used to go to Brittany for our holidays when I was young. We'd go for a couple of weeks and then grandfather Jack would pop in and say hello – and then he'd be off again. He'd have flown in, there'd be a whole commotion, and then he'd disappear almost as soon as he arrived. As a child I think I observed in him the magic of just being able to turn up and make things happen.

I started off my career with Magnet at the door factory

down in Grays, built by Mad Jack. This was part of his big expansion of the business, taking Magnet out of the north and heading south. The main business remained in Bingley and he needed to be there, but he also wanted to be on site in Essex, so he bought himself a house in Upminster and lived some of the time there. Eventually there were so many Yorkshire people going up and down to Grays that Jack built this big chalet overlooking the factory – the house that Jack built, somewhere you could stay over and have your meals. And that's where I was based when I first started as a young man – it was like a home from home. A sort of Magnet barracks. And I'd be there and then up and down to Yorkshire, just like my grandfather, all those years before.

If walls could talk, that Essex chalet would have some tales to tell.

Fast Lorries, Capable Men

Like his own father, Mad Jack was a great innovator, a risk-taker. He became president of the English Joinery Manufacturers Association, which sounds like some trumped-up, jumped-up sort of thing but which was in fact nothing of the sort. After the war, Britain was bombed out and there were a lot of displaced people with no money, and we needed to house them fast. The English Joinery Manufacturers Association, under Jack's guidance, played an important part in the reconstruction of the nation. Jack pushed the English joinery manufacturers towards standardisation – standardising the sizes of doors and windows and kitchen cabinets – because bespoke joinery just wasn't going to be able to do the job. Builders weren't able to build bespoke fast enough. Prepared manufactured joinery was the way to go. It wasn't about quality: it was about getting things done, and fast. Mad Jack was the right person for the right job at the right time.

He was a great reformer in the history of British manufacturing, Jack – though he's never really had the recognition he deserves. He also helped to break the old timber trade structure. In the old days, the trade was highly structured, to the disadvantage of the consumer. Traditionally there was an agent, who represented various sawmills, and the agent would only sell timber to you if you were a timber importer, which is to say you had to have your own dockside facilities to take the timber off the ship and store it, and then the timber importer would only sell that timber to a timber merchant, who would then sell it to local joinery works or house builders... It was a rotten system – all along that supply chain the price became inflated. So after the war, Jack managed to find someone down in Bordeaux who was prepared to ship maritime pine direct and defy the agents and the timber merchants. He was fearless, Jack.

But he was certainly no saint.

He had a henchman, Jack, a sort of fixer, who was called Harry Wright, an ex-copper, and they made quite a pair, Harry and Jack. Holy terrors. Mischief-makers. They used to drive up back to Bingley from Grays in Essex and they'd stop at the Ram Jam Inn on the A1. Mad Jack liked to drink but Harry had a monumental appetite. The story goes that one day they were in the Ram Jam Inn having lunch and Harry ordered the Aylesbury duck and they brought him the duck, which was half the duck, and he finished it, and he called the waitress over and he said, 'I'll have the other half now, please.'

And they said, you've had the duck. And he said no, it says on the menu, Aylesbury duck. It doesn't say half an Aylesbury duck. So I'll have the other half, please. So they brought him another duck, and he ate that, and off they went. Another time, Harry and Jack were at some hotel that had a ten bob luncheon buffet and it was help yourself, and so Harry did – several times. And eventually the head waiter came over and said, I don't know who you people are, but here's your ten bob back, and never come here again.

He didn't like being sold short, Jack Duxbury. He was entertaining some serious business people once at the Savoy. My mother was there, she was in her twenties. She was a sort of ornament at these occasions. And Mad Jack says to Harry, get the head waiter. I want to know why the people at the next table are eating bigger birds than we are. And off Harry goes and duly asks and the answer comes back, it's because they're having pheasants, sir, not partridges.

It's partly a West Yorkshire thing. It's partly also just being sheer bloody-minded. And it's certainly a characteristic that runs in the family. Tom Duxbury, for example – the original – was given a goat in exchange for some debt and, because everything had to earn its keep, this poor goat was kitted out with a harness to pull Tom's gardener's cart around. (As it happens, the gardener's wife got sick of the stench of goat on her husband and the goat got sold and transported up to Scotland in between a stack of windows.) My mother and her sister Kathleen were the same – nothing got past them, and everything had its price.

When he was in London, Jack liked to stay at the May Fair Hotel. On one occasion, Kathleen arrived with Harry Wright to accompany Jack to lunch, and while they were waiting, Jack appeared with a woman who was not his wife. Harry Wright, being a man of the world, said to my aunt, Miss Duxbury, I believe this young woman is helping your father with his notes. I know exactly what she's helping my father with, said my aunt. And I think you know exactly what this means for me, Mr Wright. A new fur coat. Which was duly purchased – and the matter was closed.

Jack died in 1961, aged just fifty-one, when I was seven years old. He managed to pack more into fifty years than most of us manage in a lifetime. I remember my mother saying that his average weekend consisted of coming up from King's Cross with a few drinking pals on the Bradford train, where they used to stick a newspaper on the windows of the compartment and get a couple of bottles of whisky in. Jack's driver, Tommy Holmes, would pick them up and take them to the house and they'd set themselves up in the billiard room; my grandmother would make them some sandwiches and they'd play billiards and drink until all hours. The next morning Jack would get up early and boil an egg in the kettle to save time and money and he'd walk his dogs up to a place called Dick Hudson's on Bingley Moor, where he'd stay drinking until he was picked up again, and then on Sunday he'd go to church and then get the train back down to London. Quite a routine.

He died apparently – perhaps not surprisingly – from a heart attack. He was taken to Bradford Royal Infirmary but he rang up Tommy Holmes from the hospital and Tommy came and picked him up, and Jack died at home that night.

He was a character, Jack – energetic, determined, full of ideas. He was the quintessential Duxbury. An early advertisement for the Magnet business reads, 'Fast Lorries, Capable Men' – which just about sums up the business under Jack's command.

Clogs to Clogs

The Ingle family story is a classic Yorkshire tale of clogs to clogs in three generations. What the Ingles may have lacked in Duxbury flair and flamboyance they more than made up for in diligence and determination. My success, such as it is, may well be down to a combination of the two – a lot of grit and a little bit of flair.

I suppose the real lesson of the Ingles of West Yorkshire is that family fortunes are as likely to decline and fall as they are to rise and advance, business empires as subject to decline as the great empires of nations. In business, there are no guarantees of success – but there are plenty of obvious mistakes, and I certainly learnt as much about business from the Ingles as I did from the Duxburys, both about what and what not to do.

My great-grandfather was William Law Ingle, who founded his own tannery business. William was born and grew up in Morley, which is famous for its textile industry – even to this day – and he went to school with Herbert Henry Asquith, who went on to become a politician and indeed the last British Liberal prime minister, a connection which served William well in later life. Like Asquith, William was a Methodist. He was also a serious businessman.

In 1898 William Law Ingle bought the Millshaw Works at Churwell, on the outskirts of Leeds – an enormous site. In an old local newspaper interview from around the turn of the century William Ingle – described as possessing 'bulldog features', not unlike Mad Jack – is quoted as saying that 'There is no finality in this business. If there was – if no improvements could be made, if no problems presented themselves, if no experimenting were called for, I should not have carried on. But I keep in business for the love of it – the love of fighting for supremacy. There is no greater interest.'

Dear old bulldog-featured William was as good as his word: he fought for supremacy and achieved it. W. L. Ingle – 'Tanners, Curriers and Leather Manufacturers' – eventually grew to become the biggest tannery of its kind in the country. At its height, they were tanning a million hides a year. William became the mayor of Morley, installed a chapel in the works canteen, was an enthusiastic Liberal, donated to Churwell its bowling green, tennis courts and pavilions – and happily provided leather for army boots during the First and then the Second World War, thanks in no small part to his old association with Asquith.

So, the business did well in the wars, though rather less well in times of peace. Serious problems began to emerge for W. L. Ingle in the 1960s with the advent of man-made materials and the shift towards the cheap manufacturing of shoes in the Far East. The textile and manufacturing industries in the north of England began consolidating – but rather than consolidate, W. L. Ingle dissipated, and the business eventually disappeared entirely. Opportunities were missed. Decisions were not made. Risks not taken.

My father – who eventually became Managing Director – loved the practical and theoretical side of things but wasn't really interested in the business. It just wasn't him. It wasn't his thing. Like so many war veterans, he'd done all his living during the war. He didn't have the appetite for business. He'd done his time. He'd had his adventures. He was more of an academic, a thinker. His office in the old Churwell works was the laboratory. I remember growing up around the smell of leather and chemicals – a bittersweet smell. And I can still remember the fleshing heaps where the skins were kept, and the little lizards that would come running out of the hides, and all the wild cats that were allowed to roam, to control the mice and the rats.

W. L. Ingle was a business stagnating as I grew up. It had been a great business. But it was not the business for me.

Timber!

So after my stint in the timber yards I started my management training at Magnet. They used to take on about half a dozen people a year. It was really a glorified apprenticeship. You had to spend six months in the office learning how to do accounts and debt collection, all the basic office functions. You were learning everything on the job – which is always the best way to learn. And then you went to work in the warehouse. You did sales. You did buying. You did general admin. You learnt everything about the business, and you started to get a sense of where you might like to specialise.

What I really enjoyed at Magnet was the buying – you could look at what was needed and you could ask, could we do it differently? Could we get this cheaper? Could we do it another way entirely? It was truly creative, the buying. It gave you tremendous scope to think outside the proverbial box – it suited me down to the ground.

As a trainee you also had to do a block release scheme at a place in Leamington Spa. You had to go for two-week periods at a time until you earned your credentials – there were exams and everything. One of my proudest achievements is that I became an associate of the Institute of Wood Science. I've still got the certificate somewhere.

I do love my timber. I remember the first time I went to Scandinavia, to visit our suppliers. I was just fascinated by the whole process – the wood economy, the production, the harvesting, the milling, the transportation and export, the regional and global markets, everything about it. I remember in the winters when the Baltic would ice up and you couldn't get the timber out – you'd always buy your timber subject to FOW – First Open Water. Unlikely as it sounds, there was a kind of romance to the timber trade. I've always felt it connects us to a long history of stewardship and manufacturing: good honest labour.

I eventually became a fully-fledged Magnet buyer in 1978. My boss was a man called Tony Cast. Tony was a great timber man and didn't want to give it up. Fortunately at the time we were getting more into double glazing and metal windows and plastic windows, and patio doors, and the business was growing in America, so I took a bit of a sidestep and began to expand my horizons. One of my first big successes was in the realm of window hardware, of all things – I remember I found a way to powder-coat a product so that it looked like gold. It sounds like nothing, but it was a bit of a breakthrough for me. I was on my way.

It's All Right for You, Matthew

Throughout my life people have always said to me, 'It's all right for you, Matthew.' And they're absolutely right, of course. It is all right for me. I've been very lucky.

But I've also had to make that luck. I've had to make some very difficult personal and professional decisions which have determined the course of my life and career. Sometimes I've made the right decision – sometimes not. It's been the same for me as it is for everybody else.

I have met a lot of very successful people over the years, both financially successful – people in business and finance, so-called high net worth individuals, self-made millionaires, the sons and daughters of nobility and royalty – and successful in all sorts of other ways, people living good lives and with satisfied minds, and great thinkers and doers, leaders at all levels in business and society, and plenty of everyday individuals simply blessed with uncommon insight and wisdom, people who have triumphed against the odds, the winners in life's great game. And here's what I've observed: nothing comes easy to anyone.

It's all right for you?

It's not all right for anyone.

The Sloane Square Cocktail Moment

There were several moments in my early years at Magnet that are particularly memorable – personally and professionally. One of them is what I call the Sloane Square Cocktail Moment.

A Sloane Square cocktail traditionally consists of whisky, tequila, Bénédictine and a dash of orange bitters – but without those particular ingredients to hand you can improvise with something sparkling, some orange juice and some Pimm's. However you choose to make it, I can tell you this: it's absolute dynamite.

Back in the 1980s I was working for Magnet and we were sent on one of those dreadful weekend training things – thirty of us packed off to Blackpool to be indoctrinated in the art of selling, Dale Carnegie-style. It seemed like an utterly pointless waste of time – except it wasn't.

There was a young lady on that weekend who was a PA in the company and I suggested to her one evening that we go to Trader Jack's, which was a nightclub in the old Imperial Hotel on the North Promenade – a real classy joint. She agreed to come along and I did my best to impress her. I ordered us Sloane Square cocktails. The barman had no idea how to make one, so I had to explain. We had a few, and it was one of those moments when you realise that there is no going back. It was a Sloane Square Cocktail Moment.

Anyway, dear reader, I married her.

You make a commitment, you stick to it.

Not Only Good – But Cheap

There were other successes and breakthroughs at Magnet. I remember when I met a man named Chuck Blogna, for example – again, this was the early 1980s. Meeting Chuck was one such moment. Chuck was someone who had a big impact on my thinking.

Chuck – as you might expect – was American. He made patio doors. He had a little manufacturing plant in America and I went out to visit him.

He was an extraordinary talker, Chuck – he could just talk and talk, this constant stream of chat. He was an absolute charmer. And he was also brilliant at maths – he could do the numbers very quickly in his head, just like that. Sometimes you meet those sorts of people in business, people who are really firing on all cylinders – not very often, but when you do it's worth looking and listening and observing and seeing what they have to say.

Anyway, Chuck had worked out an important principle in manufacturing – which is to always rationalise and streamline the process, to simplify at all costs, and in particular not to put a component down until you're entirely finished with it. It's basic, but if you get it right you're on to a winner. So, if you pick up a piece of metal and it's got to have holes drilled in it and then a little widget attached, don't let anyone put it down until it's had the holes drilled and the little widget attached. As soon as you introduce separate steps and stages, your costs are going to increase – and mistakes and glitches are going to occur.

Chuck had worked out how to maximise efficiencies in the manufacturing process – he had squeezed the costs, and then squeezed and squeezed again – and his patio doors were half the price of other people's. I thought this was brilliant. I came back to England and was enthusing about Chuck's patio doors, but our sales team were sceptical. They said the doors were cheap for a reason. So I invited Chuck to come over to England with his doors to show us.

I'll never forget it. Chuck arrives at Magnet HQ at Keighley – this very suave American – and right there in the middle of the boardroom he gets down on his hands and knees, takes off his jacket, and starts to put together a patio door. He was so familiar with it, he was so proud of what he'd produced, he was able to demonstrate every single stage of the process, to show us how it worked.

Not only is it good, said Chuck, it's cheap.

I took him out to dinner that evening. I had a Ford Capri 3-litre at the time and I was engaged, and I had my dog Fly. Fly was behind the seat. My fiancée was in the passenger seat, and Chuck got in the back with the dog. We went out, had a nice meal. And I remember him saying, Matthew, you are a lucky man. Your fiancée is just like Jackie Kennedy.

That was Chuck all over – good but cheap.

Tough Guys

You meet all sorts of people in business. That's why it's such fun. You meet good people – people like Chuck. People you learn from. And you meet bad people – and you learn from them too. You meet people who are very determined, who are prepared to make tough decisions, and you meet people who'll do whatever it takes to succeed. You also inevitably meet people who go that little bit too far, who cross the line.

I remember when I was a junior buyer at Magnet, doing business with someone called George Reynolds. George – well, George… In his youth he'd been put away for safecracking, handling explosives, burglary and theft. But he was also a very clever man, George, an engineer and an entrepreneur, and while he was inside, unlikely as it sounds, he figured out how to make kitchen worktops.

So I was a junior buyer, and I was always looking for leads, for new ways of doing things, and I'd heard about this bloke George Reynolds. Again, just like with Chuck Blogna, people were pretty sceptical. They warned me off, they said the quality wasn't great. George is a wrong 'un, they said. All that sort of thing. But George's worktops were significantly cheaper than the competitors. So I thought it was worth investigating – I thought I'd give the bloke a chance – and so I went to see him.

George's yard was a rough old place – it was really just a few Portakabins stuck together on a patch of wasteland. And I arrived for my appointment and walked in and there were no secretaries and no PAs. It was just George and a few lads. He struck quite a figure, George: you didn't forget George once you'd met him. He was a very well-set sort of bloke, and he had a big thick jersey on, a big gold chain round his neck – and he had his hair all long and sort of pulled across his scalp and held in place with a hair grip. It was quite a look.

Anyway, he offered me a cup of coffee and we sat down and he said, Just before we start, Matthew, do you vote Conservative? And I wasn't quite sure what to answer. I was young. He must have seen me hesitate because he went on – Let me just give you a clue, Matthew, he said. I don't supply anyone who doesn't vote Conservative. Well, in that case I definitely vote Conservative, I said. Good lad, said George, good lad. That's how George operated. Threats and suggestions – or suggestions of threats. I remember when I was leaving his yard, this Ford Granada comes screaming in as I'm about to go and it pulls up in a billow of dust and this big burly bloke leans out. Everything all right, George? Everything's fine here, says George.

He had absolutely no truck with the Labour Party, George, with lefties, or with the unions, and he didn't care who knew it. You didn't work for George if you were in a union. Matthew, he said, there was a union official who turned up here once at the yard. So I sent someone out to see him and told him to fuck right off, and this union official says he's going to get a load of people down to demonstrate outside and I said fine, go ahead, and every day you're out here demonstrating I'll tell you what I'm going to do, I'm going to fire one man per day, every day, and let's see how long you last, shall we?

Now in the end of course – inevitably – George got taken to court. George was not a good man. He was a crook. I'm not defending him.

But I would have trusted him with my life. And I will say this for him: he had worked out how to make a bloody good kitchen worktop.

The trouble with kitchen worktops is that they always get damaged on the end, so you get a lot of wastage. So George just decided he'd make his worktops three inches longer than the average size. And that was it! Problem solved.

He also only did one size, and in a strictly limited range of colours. It was a winning formula. Do you know how I select the worktop colours, Matthew? he asked. No, George, I said. I don't know how you select your worktop colours. What I do, he said, is I get the accountant in and show him all the colours you can get, and I ask him to choose the colours he likes. And he chooses. And then we select all the others. Because if the accountant likes it, we don't want it. Whatever the accountant wants, that's the opposite of what we want.

So, he simplified the whole process, George. Standard lengths, three inches longer, limited range of colours – the opposite of what an accountant might want – and he only delivered in truckloads. And he built a successful business off the back of it.

And like him or loathe him, when we got into trouble at Magnet years later, George Reynolds was the only supplier who offered to help us out – the only one. He called me direct and offered to deliver a load of worktops and we could pay him whenever we could. No strings attached...

He was a tough guy, George. Sometimes you have to do business with some pretty tough guys.

In Your Stride

There's tough, and then there's resilient, those people who just take things in their stride. I have been very lucky to have known some pretty resilient characters over the years – resilient, strong-willed and difficult, people who know their own minds and are not afraid to speak them. There was an old friend of my father's, for example, a man named Dr Pick, who became a friend and mentor to me when I was in my twenties. He was an old-school doctor, Dr Pick, but he'd also been a jockey in his youth – he'd broken his back. He walked with a stoop and a stick but he was a straight-up sort of guy.

We'd often go racing together, me and Dr Pick – greyhound racing. He had dogs which we'd take racing at Malton – the Ryedale Coursing Club. It was a pretty sketchy sort of affair, the Ryedale Coursing Club. It wasn't exactly some fancy greyhound track. There'd be a guy on a horse, and one dog with a red collar, and one with a white collar, and off they'd go, and may the best dog win.

I loved those old coursing events. You'd get all sorts there. You'd get the dog-breeders and the miners, the local toughs and the toffs, the aristocracy. It was fantastic. A real community thing. And the dogs had these big thick collars on and they were being kept on a very short lead – because once they got room for manoeuvre and got a back leg forwards, you'd never stop them. Everyone was just raring to go. Even back then in the 1970s and 1980s there was a lot of anti-behaviour, but the great thing with the coursing was that it wasn't like a hunt meet where everyone gets intimidated by the antis. At the old Ryedale coursing events people would happily take on the antis. All good clean fun. Bit of racing, bit of argy-bargy. And then you'd all retire to the pub in Thirsk. I remember I arrived back once after a day's coursing and I couldn't remember driving home.

I remember things were getting quite serious between me and my wife-to-be and I thought it was probably time she met some of my friends. So I suggested we go and see Dr Pick. Dr Pick lived near Barnsley, a place called Woolley – a nice little village. And he kept his greyhounds in his allotment behind his surgery in Barnsley. I was living in Bingley at the time so I thought we might all meet up, go for a little outing at a country fair at Chatsworth and then head over to see the greyhounds. It seemed like a good idea at the time.

I had my old Ford Capri so we picked up Dr Pick – he was sat in the front with his broken neck and my wife-to-be was in the back with Fly, my cocker spaniel. And of course as always at these events there was a massive queue to get in. Not to worry, Matthew, says Dr Pick, drive on. He had natural authority, Dr Pick – every time someone tried to stop us and flag us down he just waved his stick at them, so in the end we ended up facing the main parade ground. I remember we parked up and my wife-to-be had bunions at the time, which she foolishly mentioned to Dr Pick – we can't have that, he says. And he hauls her leg up onto the bonnet of the car. Not a problem, says Dr Pick. We'll get that cleaned up for you. Pop into the surgery Wednesday?

The rest of the day passed off more or less without incident and then we stayed overnight at Dr Pick's house, so we could get up early and go and see to the dogs the next morning. I wanted my wife-to-be to see the kennels at the allotment – a nice treat for her.

So the next morning we got up and Dr Pick was in the kitchen boiling up these bones for the dogs. The place absolutely stank. He had an old Subaru estate, Dr Pick, and after this breakfast amid the boiling bones, we piled into the car with his lurcher. I was in the back, my wife-to-be was in the front, and there was no dog guard for the lurcher, so it was all over me in the back – and then Dr Pick throws in the trough of bones and of course the dog goes absolutely mad. Dr Pick then gets behind the steering wheel but he can't move his neck because of his broken back, so he comes charging out of his driveway, in reverse, and there are cars swerving out of the way and blowing their horns and I can see my wife-to-be starting to get pretty tense up front, and then Dr Pick decides we need to go and get some eggs for the dogs, so we drive down this rough old farm track and a woman eventually comes out with a gross of broken eggs and the lurcher can smell the eggs so he's going even more frantic and it's complete mayhem in the car – we're rattling along at a hell of a speed, the dog's all over the place and howling. My wife-to-be has gone very quiet. Then we go down another farm track – to pick up some brawn. Same thing again. The dog goes mad.

So then we set off for the surgery – but not before Dr Pick announces that we need to pick up the kennel maid, so we're driving around this old Barnsley housing estate and down a cul-de-sac and it's still early in the morning but Dr Pick leans on the horn, and the dog's still leaping around, and the kennel maid eventually comes out and gets in the back with me and this half-crazed lurcher. And then we have to pick up the dog handler – same story, except this bloke comes out and gets in and he's only got one arm. And I'm thinking, what the hell is going to happen next?

Well, we get to the kennels at the allotment and somehow the dog handler gets to wrestling these greyhounds under control with his one arm and the kennel maid goes off to do her stuff, but I notice that there's this blood-stained white fur all over the fence – and guess what? It turns out that Dr Pick's greyhounds have gone and eaten the poodle next door. Oh dear, says Dr Pick. Never mind. And off he goes to sort that out. So it's early on a Sunday morning, it's total mayhem and we're out the back of this surgery on a patch of wasteland in Barnsley, and my wife-to-be is looking at me as if to say, who the hell are these people, and who are you, and then of course the Jehovah's Witnesses arrive – and rather than letting them go, Dr Pick absolutely lays into them and there's this long complicated theological argument.

All I can say is it was a very long drive back to Bingley with my wife-to-be.

Like Dr Pick, you have to learn to take things in your stride.

The Depot System

So, I'd joined the Magnet training programme in the early 1970s, then I became a buyer, we got married, and I progressed to being a senior manager. Things were going pretty well, both career-wise and family-wise.

Back then, in the 1970s and into the early 1980s, the Magnet model was a huge success – ready-made joinery and kitchens supplied to both trade and the public. And a large part of the company's success during that period – the model that eventually became the foundation, the very cornerstone of Howdens – was down to another Duxbury, my great-uncle, Philip Duxbury.

Philip was the son of my great-grandfather, the original Tom Duxbury, by Tom's second marriage. My uncle Tom Duxbury, my mother and my aunt Kathleen were the children of Mad Jack Duxbury, who was the original Tom's older son by his first marriage. So Philip was always a bit of an outsider – in terms of the business he was always playing second fiddle to my uncle Tom, but in many ways it was Philip who had inherited the entrepreneurial spirit of my grandfather Jack and the original Tom Duxbury. Just as the original Tom took a big chance with founding his firelighting business, and Mad Jack had developed standardised joinery and factories, which ensured Magnet's mid-period success, Philip was responsible for developing the depot system, the company's last great innovation.

Within the business, under my uncle Tom's direction, Philip had been hived off to a small joinery works in Birmingham, which is where he had his big idea. He realised that it would be possible to take Magnet's standardised products – the doors and windows – put them in a depot, put a price on them, and allow people to come and buy them themselves. You didn't need to waste time on marketing. You could cut out the middleman. And you could deal with your customers direct.

Before the depot system, if you were a builder and you were looking for a door, say, you had to buy from a timber merchant, who were supplied by the big importers, who were reliant on their supplies from abroad. Everything was made to order, there was a long lead time, and all along the way there were increased costs: agents, merchants, architects, clerks of works, etc, etc. But once you had standardised products, there was no reason not to sell direct to the end consumer, the builder. You piled 'em high and and you sold 'em cheap. It was really the last piece in the Magnet jigsaw – it was revolutionary.

My uncle Tom Duxbury and Philip didn't get on particularly well. Philip was a serious guy. He served as a local councillor, he was instrumental in the founding of the Yorkshire Clinic, and he was a Congregationalist: he was what I call a fundamental man. Tom was much more of a pragmatist. The two men did not often see eye-to-eye. But even Tom had to recognise the brilliance and simplicity of Phil's depot system. He backed it, and by the mid-1970s, the point at which I joined the business, we had more than a hundred depots across the country, we were extending our product range, we were building manufacturing plants, and we then joined with Southern-Evans to create Magnet & Southerns, which brought the total number of depots to more than 250 nationwide. And in 1984 we were a founding member of the FTSE 100 Share Index. There were manufacturing sites in Rotherham, Thornton, Penrith, Burnley, Deeside and Darlington. We were the country's largest joinery supplier, we had culinary showrooms. This was our heyday. We were riding high.

The Notorious MBO

Magnet's ongoing story is not mine to tell. The business is still going – if in name only. In 2001, it was bought by the Swedish kitchen manufacturer Nobia for £134 million. Nobia trades under the Magnet name in the UK, and there are still showrooms nationwide which sell kitchens to the public and the trade side of the business still supplies local builders and joiners. The business is now based in Darlington and has about 2,000 employees. It's a going concern.

But for me, the beginning of the end of my story with Magnet was around 1989 and the – infamous, the notorious – management buyout.

1989 was the beginning of the end for me – and the start of a new chapter. It was also the beginning of the end for Magnet as I had known it.

I'd gone from management trainee to trainee manager to buyer to Assistant Managing Director of Sales and in 1989 I was Head of Sales. Philip Duxbury had left the business. My uncle Tom was Chief Executive, and Tom was never satisfied. He was determined to push things forwards. He wanted to improve the fortunes of the business – and indeed his own fortune.

I had developed the idea of putting small showrooms into the depots and Tom became convinced that the future of the business was in the showrooms, in retail rather than in trade. He wanted us to develop the showrooms. He wanted the company to be registered as retail rather than as a builder – for complex financial and tax purposes.

To cut a very long story short, it was around about this point that B&Q made a bid for the business of £3 per share

– but Tom felt that this didn't give us enough money. Tom's eyes were fixed elsewhere. His dreams were set on glory. I think he felt the responsibility of his generation – to try and do something extraordinary.

Tom decided that we should mount a management buyout – we'd make a better job of running the business ourselves, he thought, rather than having to answer to pesky shareholders. We'd buy the business off the shareholders, we'd get control and all would be fine. We were the smartest people in the room, after all. Our fortunes would be secured and we'd be heroes.

I was a part of the plans. I was a part of the deal. In my early thirties I found myself for the first time dealing with the big banks and equity financiers. I was tasked with helping to find a solution. It was what you might call a steep learning curve. But we pulled it off. We achieved what Tom wanted us to achieve: we got ourselves some serious loans to buy the company. We took out loans worth about £700 million. Which was a lot of money. This was at a time when the profitability of the company was only about £40 million. And so the management buyout went ahead.

And then – pretty much as soon as we had secured the loans – interest rates shot up to 15 per cent. Overnight, we owed the bank more in interest than we could possibly afford. Life's like that. It has a way of changing the odds. You just can't see that far down the road.

Interest rates shot up. And then the recession hit.

1989 turned out to be a completely mad year – a very bad year – for everyone at Magnet.

In January 1989 we had announced plans for the management buyout.

By the summer we had pulled it off: what was at the time the biggest management buyout in British corporate history.

And by October we were struggling to repay the interest rates. Staff were put on short-time.

In the space of a year we'd gone from heroes to zeroes. You can look it all up in the newspapers. It makes for grim reading.

It was all too much for Tom. By early 1990 he had resigned and gone to Switzerland. The banks took over, and a man named John Foulkes was brought in to try and save things. A series of holding companies were put in place and then in January 1994 Magnet was bought by Berisford International. I'd hung on as long as I could, but a few months later I was out.

In fairness, it had been quite a run of success. Founded after the First World War by Tom Duxbury as a one-man firewood company, which then developed into the old ammo-box chicken shed business, and then into general joinery, and then the standardised joinery of Mad Jack, and the factories and Philip's depots, the FTSE 100. Magnet was a great company – until it wasn't. It lives on – but it's not the same.

Give Me the Figures

With big companies with long histories, no one involved can ever quite believe that things are going to go badly wrong. No one ever thinks a big business is going to fail. It just seems impossible. The bigger the business, the more inevitable they seem – Woolworths, Debenhams, Kodak. They're just *there*. No one ever thinks they're going to collapse. But things do collapse. Things do go wrong. Terrible things happen. Businesses fail.

For me the moment I realised that we were in serious trouble at Magnet was around October 1989 – the MBO had gone ahead, we'd bought the business, interest rates were rocketing, the market was collapsing and I remember I asked the accounts department how much money we had in the bank. I'll never forget what they said. *It's not as simple as that, Matthew* – that's what they said. *It's not as simple as that.* But surely we can just ring up and ask the bank how much money we have, I said. It's not as simple as that, they said. It's more complicated. There are some funds coming in and some funds going out. It's not as simple as that.

In other words, they couldn't answer the question.

In business, when someone can't answer the question, when you can't get a straight answer, you know that you are in serious trouble. Because at the end of the day there is a straight answer to the question of how much money you have in the bank. You've either got this or you've got that. It's not complicated.

Of course in life some things are complicated: people can be complicated, relationships can be complicated, big ideas in philosophy and science and religion can be complicated. We all face complications in our lives every day. But the basic principles of business, of management, of finance and of leadership are all pretty simple. The biggest challenge in business, as in life, is keeping things simple – like staying on top of your finances, day after day, month after month and year after year after year.

From the moment when things at Magnet started to go so terribly wrong, I decided I was always going to know the exact figures – how much we made, how much we had, how much we didn't have, *every single day*. And I did. At Magnet, and then at MFI and at Howdens, I would get the figures every day, at the close of play. At Howdens, the depots would ring the area manager and then the regional manager and then I'd get the figures from the operations manager. What

I wanted to know was very simple. What I wanted to know from the managers was what they had sold today and what they thought they were going to sell tomorrow – that's all. I didn't want to look at the figures on a graph on a computer. I wanted to hear it direct, from the managers, every day.

Why? Why was this so important? Because it makes people take ownership. It's important that people actually say it. It has to be articulated – and it needs to be heard. So that everyone can understand – and so there's no misunderstanding. It doesn't really matter if the numbers are up or down – saying them makes you think about them. And hearing them makes me think about them. Knowing the actual figures is about dealing with the facts – not fairy stories, facts.

I kept a record of our daily figures in the back of my diary for years and years, so that if anyone ever asked me about our figures I could show them. I had it immediately to hand. I would show them the back of my diary. I showed it to our bankers and to our investors. You want to know our figures? Fine. Here they are. Right here in the back of my diary. Here are today's numbers. And yesterday's, and the day before that and the day before that.

I wish everyone kept a diary like that, said one investor.

Me too. I wish someone had kept a diary like that at Magnet.

Stout Fellow

So, it was late 1989. I had a serious decision to make.

The MBO had been a disaster. We owed the banks £700 million. Philip Duxbury was gone. Tom Duxbury was going.

I was the last Duxbury descendant in the business. There was a board meeting and I remember on the way in, Will Samuel – who I regarded as our de facto chairman, having been brought in as Schroders' lead merchant banker – asking me what I was going to do. Was I going to stay or was I going to leave? Would I stay or would I go?

I'll be honest. It was a difficult decision. I'd really had to think things through. And it was a genuine choice. I could have cut and run with all the others. I could have taken the money and started all over again somewhere else. It was a possibility. I was tempted to do so. I'd be lying if I said I didn't think about it. I could have taken a very different path.

But I didn't. For me, for better or worse, it was a matter of principle.

So, what are you going to do? asked Will Samuel. I had thought about it. I had wrestled with it. I had discussed it with my wife.

I am going to stay, I said. I am going to stay and I am going try to put things right, and I'm going to build a reputation.

Stout fellow, said Will. Stout fellow. And that was the end of the conversation.

It was the right thing to do.

It was also a difficult thing to do. I had a mortgage and school fees to pay. I was effectively losing everything. I was turning down a payout and losing my stake in the business. But I said I'd stay, and I did. I took a big pay cut, and then I had to do some pretty quick thinking. I needed to come up with a plan.

Magnet had clearly lost its way. We'd lost the run of ourselves. There were shops, there were showrooms. We were all trying to do too much. So I came up with a plan.

I said we needed to split the business into trade and retail. It wasn't an idea that came out of long-term planning or thinking.

It was just facing things as they were, in the moment. If we split the business into trade and retail, I reasoned, that would give them both a chance. And because, despite the mess, I'd just run the best winter sale we'd ever had, John Foulkes, our new Chief Executive, was prepared to listen to me – and agreed that I should start running the trade business from 1 February 1990. It was a massive opportunity – for me and for the business. I was off the leash. I'd be able to do things the way I thought they should be done. I'll always be grateful to John for that.

So we split the business into two and from that moment, things began to improve.

I was lucky. New horizons opened up for me. Magnet survived – but the old Magnet was finished.

Stout fellow? Maybe. Simply doing the right thing.

The Towpath

When we were first married our house was this little cottage on the Leeds and Liverpool Canal in East Marton, and people would walk past on the towpath. And something struck me one day, as I was looking out – people either walked one way, or the other. Again, it's entirely obvious. But it's always taken me time to realise the importance of the obvious. The thing about a towpath is this: there are only two directions. The way you've come, and the way you're going.

Most people like to give their opinions endlessly about things. They have all sorts of ideas. But there are really only two questions.

Where are you going? And where have you been?

Hold on to the Wreckage

It's funny, the impact of just a few words at the right time. I remember in the early spring of 1990, when so much was still hanging in the balance – splitting the business into two, the restructuring, working out the debt refinancing – I received a phone call from a man named John Carter. John was from a big brewing family in Sheffield and he owned and ran a greyhound stadium. I knew him from my greyhound coursing days. He was a friend of Dr Pick and he'd gone to school with my uncle Tom Duxbury. He'd heard what had been happening at Magnet and decided to get in touch.

John was a very lively character – you could listen to him talk for hours. John always knew the answer. And if he didn't, he'd convince you that he did. (The story goes that he was left with one of his children once, when they were just a baby, and he couldn't get them off to sleep, so he mixed up a bottle of hot chocolate with some whisky. Which certainly meant the baby went to sleep – the problem was the mess when they woke up.)

Anyway, John basically invited himself to lunch, completely out of the blue. We had no facilities at the Magnet office for dining and in Keighley back then you weren't exactly spoilt for choice so I decided to take him a few miles down the road to Steeton, to a very nice old pub called the Goat's Head. We had lunch and we chatted about a few things and eventually we got round to talking about what was happening at Magnet. And this is what he said. It was a throwaway remark really, but it absolutely hit the target. Matthew, he said, the best advice I can give you is to hang on to the wreckage. (He also

Hold on to the Wreckage.

said that having known Tom from his schooldays he wasn't at all surprised that he'd taken off for Switzerland. He knew my uncle all too well.)

Hang on to the wreckage: good advice.

If you hang on to the wreckage, you might be able to repair things. You might be able to put things right. But if you give it all up and go off on your own, goodness only knows what might happen.

I remember shortly before he died, Philip Duxbury sent me a lovely letter – he said he always thought that I had it in me to be a great businessman, like the original Tom Duxbury. Philip understood that to succeed in business you often need to be unreasonably determined – bold, brave, knuckle-headed. Not only do you have to be able to do a deal, for example, you have to be able to do a big deal, under pressure, and then cope with all the fallout and the consequences, good and bad. And if something seems unfixable and broken beyond repair, first you need to see if you can fix it.

The Golden Rule

I know that these are hardly revelatory insights. But in business you're always learning and discovering the basic truths, again and again – deep truths. It's like buried treasure, or fossils in the ground, the statue inside the marble: it's all just there, waiting to be unearthed and rediscovered.

My wife's uncle Malcom Shuttleworth had a lovely small hotel in Pitlochry. In his youth he'd been a grocer – he had a small shop – but one day, so the story goes, he was at Hull

The golden rule of business

docks, picking up his supplies in his little van, and a big truck arrived, and in that moment he realised that he was never going to be able to compete at that sort of scale. So he took himself off to Scotland and reinvented himself as a hotelier. He and his wife had this modest little place, a few rooms, nothing grand, and I can remember the first time I visited with my wife there was a sign in reception, just as you walked through the door, a reminder to guests as much as to staff. The sign was titled 'The Golden Rule in Business', by Reverend James L. Gordon. It always stuck in my mind, and years later I asked Malcom's daughter to write it down. As a rule, it is hard to beat.

The GOLDEN RULE is the world's standard of fairness, of honesty, of impartiality, of honour, squareness and rectitude. Can it be applied in business? And I answer that question by asking this question. Can any other rule except the GOLDEN RULE be applied in business? Is there any other rule by which anything worthy of the title of business can be achieved? Is there any business in rascality? Is there any business in meanness? Is there any business in low cunning? Is there any business in poor work? Is there any business in low quality? Is there any business in short measure? When a man throws his conscience overboard, is that a business transaction? Is a shyster a businessman? Is a crook a businessman? Is a father a businessman? Is a grafter a businessman? Is double dealing to be classed as business? What is business? I will give you a definition of business to which the GOLDEN RULE is the only rule that can be applied. Business is a service rendered, the quality and worth of which equals the price charged and admits of a fair profit. That is business. It seems to me that if we are to have anything worthy of the name, title and appellation of business, there is only one thing that will meet it and match it: there is only thing for a foundation and that is the GOLDEN RULE: 'Do unto others as you would have others do unto you.'

Be Prepared

I've met a lot of people in business over the years who have never quite grasped the importance of the Golden Rule – a lot of them are bankers. But I've also met plenty who have instinctively understood it. John Stephenson was one of them.

John and his family owned a hardware shop on North Street in Darlington – I used to buy screws from them when I was at Magnet. It was a proper old-fashioned hardware store. You'd go in and ask for a sharpening stone, and – just a moment, sir – that'd be it, there's your sharpening stone, sir. And not only that, but which of our sharpening stones is the most suitable for your purposes, sir? It was a proper shop, the Stephenson's family shop in Darlington.

Over the years the business grew, so that they didn't just supply sharpening stones for local builders and DIY enthusiasts – they also supplied drill bits to the oil rigs in the North Sea. The Stephensons could get you anything you wanted. The story goes that one day they answered a call and it was someone looking for a Mercedes-Benz fire engine. I'll see what I can do, sir. And sure enough, in three days, a Mercedes-Benz fire engine was duly delivered.

Anyway, every week John Stephenson would come and visit

the storekeeper for our factories. Storekeepers are relatively low down in the pecking order of a business – but John was smart. He knew that even if the storekeeper didn't know that he needed something, he might need it, and so he had to have it. He'd go round the stores and check that we had not only what we needed for the following week but for the week after that and the week after that and the week after that – and that we had in stock those things that we didn't even know we were going to need in stock. John was one of those people who took care of things: he made sure we were always well prepared, even when we didn't know that we needed to be well prepared.

You have to have everything there when it's required. Not most of it. All of it.

Face the Facts

Anyway, going back to dear old John Carter's advice – it took some doing to hold on to the wreckage and to try and make things good at Magnet.

We really were in an unholy mess and it was basically just me and John Foulkes there trying sort it all out. One of the things we needed to do was to find a new chairman. Which was quite a task. We were a basket case. No one wanted to touch us. But cometh the hour...

Louis Sherwood was a lovely man. Friendly, determined. A person of great integrity. And he had a brilliant mind. He'd read classics at Oxford, then studied in America and gone into business – financial services, retail. He'd done it all. He went on to become the chairman of HTV, the broadcaster. He was very outspoken, very tall and massively energetic – he was constantly rocking backwards and forwards in his chair, Louis. It didn't take him long to work his way through a chair.

The thing about Louis was that he absolutely detested bankers. His basic position was, don't believe a word they say. Don't trust them: *whatever* they say, don't trust them. After my experience with Magnet, and later with MFI, I'd say he was about right.

Anyway, Louis came on board as chairman – thank goodness. His other big theme – apart from Don't Trust Bankers – was Face the Facts. Whatever the facts are, Louis would say, just deal with them. We were carrying a lot of stock at Magnet, far too much. I remember going round a depot with him and he was examining everything very carefully. What's this? he'd say. Oh, it's this or that, I'd say. It's got a lot of dust on it, he'd say. So it's clearly been hanging around a while. Are you sure you're going to sell it? Oh yes, I'd say. But you couldn't fool Louis. He knew when things needed to be done, when action needed to be taken. Look, Matthew, he said, you've got enough trouble to deal with already. If you're not going to sell it, just get rid of it. Forget it. Write it off. Give it away if you have to. Skip it. Do whatever you have to do. Because if it's not selling, it's not selling. Don't kid yourself. Face the facts.

I have been very lucky over the years – a lot of people I've worked with have been seriously bright people, from foremen in the yards, from Johnny Jagger at JPA, all the way up to our chairmen at Howdens. But the people I really admire are those who are prepared to tell the truth, who are courageous and steadfast under extreme pressure and provocation. If you work with those sorts of people you'll be OK. If you work with those sorts of people it's extraordinary what you can achieve. Louis Sherwood was one of them. Most people have things they want to do or make happen – but they're not prepared to face the facts. You can think or feel whatever you like. But the facts are facts, and they have to be faced.

Salvage

I must admit, I enjoyed helping to steer us through those difficult times at Magnet. I found it stimulating and rewarding – it just suited me.

When I was younger I used to think that I might have liked to have worked in forestry – something useful, something outdoors. Good, hard, honest physical labour. So it's probably no accident that I started out in timber yards and that my life has been spent working with wood.

In recent years I've thought more about what I might otherwise have done – and what I still might do. I know myself a little better now. And I think if I had my time again – maybe even now it's not too late – I might like to be the skipper of my own salvage tug. A proper f*** off salvage tug – something substantial.

I'd have it moored somewhere up near Greenock, get myself a crew together, and we'd loll and loiter about and eat and drink and wait for something to happen. And when it did – appalling weather, some disaster – we'd fire up the old engine and batten down the hatches, plot the course, and off we'd go. Radio silence. The South China Sea. The Arctic. The Barents.

All we'd need to do is just get in range – and then a quick call to Lloyds. We have the tanker in sight. We await your instructions.

I like the idea that I might be able to save stricken vessels.

Anchors

It's all very well being a buccaneering salvage man, but amid all the inevitable storms and chaos of life you do need some anchors. Anchors are very important.

Some people find their anchors in the church or in religion, or in alcohol or drugs or goodness knows what. For me, my anchors have always been my wife, my family, my dogs, and my home in Yorkshire. I'll be honest, without my wife, I'd be entirely adrift – though I'm sure she'd say I still am.

I'm very lucky, because my wife used to work as a PA – though not for me – so she knows how to deal with PAs. I remember years ago, for example, she got a phone call at home from a PA in some department or other when I was working with MFI – we understand that Matthew's going to this or that or the other, and we just need to know exactly when and where he's going. My wife just put the phone down. It was none of their business. It was Howdens' business.

Another time, we were at Gleneagles and there was a big refinancing meeting we had to get to in London but there was some sort problem with the trains and the planes and I had a group of three or four people with me. I said, We'll make it down there somehow, and so we organised a car and just started driving south. I rang my wife. By the time we'd got to the outskirts of Edinburgh she'd got us on a little plane to take us down to London City Airport. Done.

On another occasion we'd organised some sort of work away day and we were doing some hovercrafting and I said to the guy with the hovercraft, when we get out there nothing will go wrong, will it? Like what? he said. Well, let's just imagine, I said. What if we sink? It won't sink, he said, it's a sealed hull. Are you sure, I said? He was absolutely sure. And sure enough, we were out in the middle of this lake, and bang, something went wrong. Don't worry, he said, everything's fine. I said I'm not worried, I can swim. And there was someone dispatched in a rowing boat to pick us up. But he broke a rollock, so he was going round and round in circles and then another boat came slowly paddling out – but by then I could hear the tell-tale sound of trickling water. It looks to me like we're settling in the water, I said. No no, said the captain. We're going to be fine. And then suddenly we were sinking. The captain starts shouting and yelling. My wife was on the shore. People were panicking. What about Matthew? Don't worry, she said. It won't kill him. And it didn't. Of course it didn't. We all just swam to shore.

Anchors.

Play Dominoes

In business you need to trust others. And you need to be trusted by others. How? How do you gain trust and respect? You do it by building relationships. You can't fake it. You have to spend time with people and gain their trust.

I'll tell you what you have to do: you have to play dominoes.

That's not a metaphor. I mean actual dominoes – you need to play dominoes.

You need to understand that back in the 1970s and 1980s people would still go for a drink at lunchtime. Everybody did. It was common practice. At Magnet, the directors of the company would have lunch served in the boardroom, while the rest of us, from the foremen and the lads in the yard all the way up to the general managers, would go for a pint in the local pub, the Airedale Heifer in Keighley, and play penny a spot. It wasn't exactly an extensive menu in the Airedale Heifer – mostly pie and peas from what I remember – and most of the lads would be drinking beer, but I was never much of a beer drinker, so I'd order wine, which would come in a half pint glass. That certainly made for an easier afternoon. Simpler times. And we'd have a game of dominoes. I enjoyed playing dominoes with the lads.

And then in the autumn of 1989, when the management buyout had gone wrong, it was the Magnet foremen's do. If you got invited to the foremen's do you knew you were right well in, as we used to say. And I was lucky enough to have been invited. Now, people's jobs were on the line; there was a lot of dissatisfaction and upset. I had obviously been a part of the whole thing and was identified as part of the boss class and I thought there was no way I'd be invited to the foremen's do. But I was invited, and when I was invited I wondered if I should go, because I knew everyone would be wanting to ask me questions and there might be a lot bad feeling, but I knew that if I didn't go that'd be worse. It would be sending the wrong signal. So I went.

And it was a good old-fashioned dominoes drive – a knock-out competition. I can't remember exactly what you won, but people really fought for it. There was an all-you-can-eat buffet – a great buffet – and you could only drink beer or lager till 10.30 p.m., but then between 10.30 and 11 you could drink as many shorts as you liked.

And do you know what?

No one said a word about the management buyout – not a single person. It was just an enjoyable night out, a few drinks, a few laughs. It was testament to the kindness and good nature of the workforce at Magnet – and of all those lunches we'd spent together at the Airedale Heifer playing dominoes.

Hengist and Horsa

So, 1990.

Having come up with the idea of a split between the trade and retail business, various consultants were called in to help us work out exactly how to do it – L.E.K., A. T. Kearney, the big consultancy firms.

And in the end, it was decided that John Foulkes would run the retail business and I would run trade. Everyone thought that the trade business would fail – and a lot of people thought that having been part of the management buyout that was exactly what I deserved. Even the consultants were sceptical. I remember one of the L.E.K. consultants saying, Matthew, I don't think you're going to get very far with this. And I said, remember Hengist and Horsa? He said, Whogist and Whosa? He was American. He didn't have a clue what I was talking about. Hengist and Horsa – the two legendary brothers who led the Angles, Saxons and Jutes in the invasion of Britain in the fifth century. That's what it was like, for a brief moment. We were battling together. And it really was a battle. It was a battle for survival.

My first job was going round the Magnet depots, persuading staff that despite the MBO mess we knew what we were doing, that the Magnet Trade business was still worth fighting for, and that as a business we were committed to guaranteeing good quality at low costs – with fewer people employed. It was a pretty tough undertaking. It wasn't exactly pleasant. We were often having to run depots with just two people – which was not ideal for anyone. And I had to tell people that their contracts were going to be renegotiated. There's no easy way to tell people that.

I had to get our managers on board. I remember once I got all fifty of our senior managers together and I told them that we had to think of ourselves – unlikely as it sounds, since we were essentially just a bunch of entirely ordinary English lads and lasses – as proud Viking warriors, running up a beach, swords in hands, determined to triumph because there was no going back, because we'd burnt our boats. It was the first time I used the Viking warrior example, but it certainly wasn't the last. In later years I was given a plaque to commemorate my various Viking warrior speeches – they were always taken in good part, the speeches, and maybe they were slightly tongue-in-cheek, but they were also true. In business you really are in a battle for your survival, and the only way to go is forwards – in which case you'd better be prepared to burn all the boats.

Hard Lessons for Tough Times

In the end, with John Foulkes at Magnet, we got so far, but no further. I learnt some hard lessons from John – as did the whole business. He taught me three very important principles which I took with me into my work at Howdens.

1. **Cash is King** If you've got it, you're fine. If you haven't, you're not – because no one is going to want to lend you the money, and if they do, guess what, you're going to have to pay it back, with interest and more. You need to run a cash generative business. Cash is King.

2. **Lowest Cost Production** Is not a nice-to-have, it's a must-have. If you don't have the lowest cost production you are going to find someday that someone else will, and someday someone is going to reduce their prices, and if you can't match them, you are going to be in serious trouble. One day, like it or not, you are going to have to get into the gutter with a competitor and you had better be sure that you're the one who is going to be able to crawl back out again, because only one of you is going to survive. Sorry. I know it sounds awful, but it's true.

3. **Your Best is Not Good Enough** I would sometimes say to John that we were doing our best at this or that and he would simply say, Matthew, that is not an argument. It doesn't matter whether you're doing your best or not. In business you're not rewarded for good efforts. Sometimes your best is not going to be good enough.

These were hard lessons for tough times. The recession

of the early 1990s hit Magnet hard. More and more things started to go wrong – there was a long-running industrial dispute, a lack of investment, and then Berisford International took over and they wanted to merge trade back with retail. I disagreed rather strongly. I thought we should keep trade and retail separate.

A few months' later, in July 1994, I was fired.

Head Hunters and Hyenas

For the first time in my life I was without work.

Though not for long.

First I was approached by Jewson, the builders' merchants – they were looking for a Chief Executive. I met the executive board and the chairman. I liked the look of them. They seemed to like the look of me. Everything was going really well – until I was asked which university I went to. I didn't go to university. And that was that, the deal was off.

That shook me up. That got me thinking.

I then went to see a head hunter in Edinburgh. It was a very useful meeting. Indeed, in some ways it was a pivotal meeting. It confirmed what I already knew, and what my recent experience with Jewson had proved. We talked for some time, he listened to what I was saying, and he made an observation – this was just on the basis of one meeting. How long, Matthew, he asked, do you think it would be before you realised that the new person you're working for is an absolute idiot, and how long before the person you're working for realises that you're a complete hyena?

He was a wise man, that head hunter. He had a point.

I needed a plan – my own plan.

I needed to think about what I really believed and what I wanted to do.

Skipton Market Rules

Here's what I believe. Skipton Market Rules.

These three words pretty much sum up my entire business philosophy.

Skipton – in case you don't know – is a fine market town in North Yorkshire, north of Leeds, west of York, Gateway to the Dales. There's a castle. There's the Leeds and Liverpool Canal. And there's the market – Mondays, Wednesdays, Fridays and Saturdays. There is nothing you can't get at Skipton Market – clothes, fruit and veg, meat, cheese, household goods, tools, stationery, plants and flowers. You name it, you can get it. Plus a lot of good cheer. It's a day out, Skipton Market.

Over the years, when people have asked me why I did this or that in business or why I didn't do some other thing, I'd always say, Skipton Market Rules.

Skipton Market Rules.

First, you've got to make money – that's the number one priority. Any business, no matter how big, is really just like a market stall – you're offering people something to buy, and if they want to buy it, you're fine. If not, you're in trouble. It's as simple as that. Nothing else counts – it's about making money. And, by the way, it's got to be real money. Actual money, that you get to put in your pocket at the end of the day – not funny

Skipton Market Rules.

1. Make money.
Ensure you have more money at the end of the day than you started with.

2. Be the best.
Always turn up, sell good produce, be answerable to your every decision.

3. Remember It's your stall.
Do your own thing, specialise.

4. Your reputation.
we've got all the time in the world to build a reputation... so no time to lose.

money, and not someone else's pocket. It's pretty simple: do you have more money at the end of the day than you had at the start? If you do, you're following Skipton Market Rules. You get up early, set out your stall, do your business, pack up and go home – and at the end of every day there's a moment of reckoning. Am I making money?

Second, if you're running a stall on Skipton Market, you'd better make sure you're bloody good at it. If you're selling apples, you need to be the best apple-seller on the market, offering the customer exactly what they want, at the right price, day in, day out, come rain or shine. You'd better enjoy it, because you can't decide not to turn up one week. If you're not there, you're going to lose your customers to a more reliable apple-seller and pretty soon you're not going to have a business. Oh, and you can't sell bad apples either, because your customers are going to come back to you next week to complain – and then go to your competitor. And you can't rip them off, because you're going to be there, on Skipton Market, you're going to be living and working among the people you serve, and so you're going to have to be answerable for your every decision. Skipton Market Rules.

Finally, you need to remember that you're running your stall and not someone else's. If I had my apple stall on Skipton Market and I'd been selling fantastic apples for years and you came to me and said you wanted some lemons I'd just point you in the direction of the bloke or the woman a few stalls down who does lemons. There'd be no point in me trying to get into selling lemons because it would divert my time and effort from what I do best – which is selling apples. You might say, Oh but Matthew, you're so good at selling apples, I'm sure you'd be great at selling lemons. Well, I might be, but it would take me years to become an expert lemon-seller and I'd have to take my eye off my apple business in order to do so. So thank you, but no thank you. I'll do my thing – I'll look after my stall – and I'll let other people look after theirs. Skipton Market Rules.

Do something that you're good at, that makes money, that gives the customer what they want, when they want it, and at the right price, and for goodness' sake DO NOTHING ELSE. That's Skipton Market Rules.

'Tha'd better come and see me, son'

I was free from Magnet for the first time since my teens. I was free to think and free to act. What did I really want to do? Who did I want to be? What did I want to become?

I was lucky. It didn't take me long to work it out.

I'd been in trade my whole life. I loved the trade business. I loved everything about it. It was in my blood and my bones. And I realised that with Magnet moving back towards a retail model there was a gap in the market when it came to supplying the building trade. A nationwide network of no-nonsense, value-sensitive trade depots where local builders could pick up exactly what they needed from stock to get their jobs done quickly.

It was a very simple idea. It was basically Philip Duxbury's depot system, reborn. For me, with my background and experience, it didn't take much working out.

I wrote a letter to Derek Hunt, who was then MFI's Managing Director, and explained to him that I had an idea.

The letter was dated 31 October 1994.

Derek kindly called a few days later and uttered the memorable words, 'Tha'd better come and see me, son.'

And that was the beginning of Howdens.

The £100M Trade Opportunity

The document I put together to show Derek Hunt was only a few pages long. I titled it – optimistically, but not without foundation – 'The £100M TRADE OPPORTUNITY'.

'The purpose of this report is to establish if [I left this blank in my early drafts of the document, in case I had to hawk it around] can develop a trade proposition as successful as its current retail offering.'

I then addressed what I thought were the major opportunities and challenges facing my proposed business – the size of the market, the product, the distribution, human resources – and a brief business plan, including a twelve-month plan and a three-year forecast.

I reckoned the business might be worth £100 million.

It turned out to be an underestimate.

Dear Mr Hunt

If there is a single person responsible for the success of Howdens, it is Derek Hunt.

Derek was an absolutely extraordinary individual: if anyone might be described as a larger-than-life character, it was Derek. He began his working life as a policeman and was often referred to by colleagues as DSH, partly because of his middle name, Simpson, and partly because he retained throughout his career the no-nonsense manner and approach of a tough detective sergeant. You didn't mess with Derek.

He was originally from Darlington, Derek, and started working in retail with BHS, and then with Fine Fare before joining MFI as retail director and going on to become Chief Executive. It was Derek who led MFI in its heyday and who organised the big management buyout in 1987, after an unhappy merger with Asda. He remained chairman of MFI until he retired in 2000, and he died in 2012. One of the few regrets I have is that Derek wasn't around to see the massive success of Howdens – he never got to see what he and I imagined in the early days eventually become a reality.

Derek was what you might call a man's man. He was massive – huge. He always had a twinkle in his eye. He smoked like a chimney – a whole stack of chimneys – drank like a shoal of fish, and loved a bit of a flutter. If you went out with Derek for a night out it was a proper night out. You never quite knew where you'd end up, or how.

There are dozens of stories about Derek. I remember he rang his wife one morning – you'll never guess where I am, he said. In the pub? she said, knowing Derek. Prague, he said. There was another time he flew over to Jeddah and his baggage was lost. There were no suits big enough over there to fit him, so he spent the entire trip in one of those white Saudi tunics, a thobe – this big, white, flush-faced giant of a man. Quite a sight. We were also in Taiwan once and were being entertained by clients; they started drinking some local spirit and I soon started to feel pretty rough, but Derek leaned across and said, I'll take it from here, son – he always called me son – and then proceeded *literally* to drink them under the table. I've never seen anything like it. We were meant to be having a meeting the following morning. I don't think there's going to be a meeting in the morning now, said Derek. And we got up and left, leaving these Taiwanese guys floored. Literally floored. He was a steam engine of a man.

As it turned out, I couldn't really work with Derek – we were far too alike. But I absolutely adored him. Derek was one of those people, once he'd decided something was going to happen, it was going to happen. We'd both been through management buyouts, and so he knew how people behaved under pressure. He understood it all: the anger, the hurt, the frustration, the appalling behaviour of bankers. We'd fought the same wars. We'd experienced the same thing.

Anyway, Derek saw what I'd done at Magnet – so when I turned up to meet him he knew I was a ready prospect. He decided to back me, there and then. Go ahead, he said. See if you can get a trade business going through MFI. He gave me access to all the facilities and resources at MFI – we were turbo-charged before we got going.

Derek gave me my big break – as he did with so many others. Derek was really one of the founders of Howdens.

I always tell people that the real moment of victory for Howdens was not when we got to £1 a share, or when we made this much profit, or had so many depots or staff. The real moment of victory was when Derek Hunt came into our Kingston depot in April 1996, six months after we had started trading, and he walked up and down for a bit and just said, detective sergeant-style, 'If this works, Matthew, it's going to be bigger than Brink's-Mat.' He didn't need to see anything else, or say anything else – he just got back in his Rolls-Royce, in a cloud of smoke, and drove away. With his approval, with his backing, with his signature, everything worked. From that moment on, Howdens never looked back.

I still have a copy of the letter I wrote to him on 31 October 1994, from our old house near Keighley, which is where it all began.

Dear Mr Hunt

Managing Director – Magnet Trade

Since the change of ownership, the above position which I used to hold is redundant. I can't work, for contract reasons, until 1st January 1995.

Having heard a lot about you, it would be nice to meet you sometime. Although I don't think you will be interested in anything I have to say about retailing, I believe I have a proposition which could add substantially to your sales, and I would welcome an opportunity to discuss this with you.

I will telephone your secretary next week.

Yours sincerely,

Matthew Ingle.

If Derek hadn't replied, or if he hadn't been prepared to take a chance on me, there would be no Howdens.

So, Derek Hunt brought me into the business, but in a sense he also saw me out.

Derek retired at sixty, while the going was still good. One of the most important lessons I learnt from him was that your day in the sun does not last forever. Look, son, he said, you need to know when to go.

The Howdens business owes an awful lot to Derek. I owe him everything, including his final gift to me: knowing when it's time to go.

Rock-Solid MFI

Without MFI, launching Howdens wouldn't have been possible. They had the supply base, they had the offices, the systems, the experts, everything that I could possibly hope for to try and kickstart a business.

MFI, in case you didn't know – Mullard Furniture Industries – was founded in 1963. At first, it simply sold affordable furniture by mail order. It then began to specialise in fitted kitchen units and bedroom furniture and in 1967 it opened a major showroom in Wembley. It became a great British success story, a seemingly permanent feature of every out-of-town retail park – so much so that it used to be said that one in three of all Sunday lunches in the UK were made in MFI kitchens and over 60 per cent of British children conceived in an MFI bedroom.

MFI was rock-solid. MFI provided the foundation on which Howdens was built. Howdens began as a part of the MFI group – a big public company – and succeeded because of MFI. And then, eventually, when MFI was faltering, I am very proud to say that Howdens shouldered the burden in return – for the pensioners, the shareholders, the MFI landlords. We did the right thing. They supported us. We supported them. What goes around comes around.

Houdan? Howden? Howdens

I had Derek Hunt's backing. I had the full power of MFI behind me.

What I didn't have was a name for this brave new trade business I'd dreamt up.

I'd joined MFI in April 1995. We'd agreed we'd be opening our first depots by October. It was now July – and we still didn't have a name.

I kept coming up with different ideas. Names were going round and round in my mind, but nothing sounded quite right.

I knew that I wanted something that sounded solid and reliable and traditional – a name that sounded like it had been around for a while. I wanted a down-to-earth, no-nonsense, British-sounding sort of name that people could relate to. I wanted a name that suggested times past and which gave the impression of a company with a historical manufacturing base... I wanted it to be perfect.

I spent a lot of time thinking about the name – names are important. They tell us who we are. And they tell other people who we think we are. I knew that I had one chance to get it right.

I remember I would sit in the Angel Inn at Hetton with my wife; there were all these pictures on the wall and we'd free-associate and come up with things, stuff to do with nature, stuff to do with animals. Beaverwood Joinery? How about that? No. Something to do with bees? Hives? No. MFI had a factory in Runcorn – maybe we could have something to do with corn? No. Sheaves? No. None of it worked.

And then one day we were visiting my sister-in-law and she had this Victorian print of hens on the wall – and I

The Company name

HOUDEN × HOWDEN × HOWDENS ˅

Heritage values

Craft

Community

HOWDENS
JOINERY CO.

remember I was looking at the names of these traditional breeds of chickens. The Norfolk Grey. The Scots Dumpy. The Lincolnshire Buff. None of them quite right. But one of them was a Houdan – Poule de Houdan, a French hen. The Houdan. It was one of those moments. I've lived in Yorkshire all my life and the village of Howden was nearby, which also happened to be the home of Hygena Ltd, a kitchen manufacturer which had become part of the MFI group of companies. Houdan. Howden. Everything suddenly came together, just like that. Houdan? Howden? Howden*s* – the added s seemed to allow the name to roll off the tongue that little bit easier. And just like that, the name was decided.

What's the American saying, 'Don't sweat the small stuff?' Sometimes you do sweat the small stuff. But you can sweat it all you like – sometimes the answer just falls into your lap. Do the work, be diligent – and be prepared for surprises.

Signs and Symbols

Of course, all business is fundamentally about making money by producing – or buying and selling – goods and services. Skipton Market Rules. That's what business is about.

But it's not *just* about buying and selling. It's about producing value. Products represent ideas and feelings: we buy certain products because we want to feel a certain way. This is why symbols are so important – because they signify ideas and feelings. Symbols are signals: friend or foe, stop or go. Symbols help to us navigate our way through the world. They help us to think. They create associations. They bring us together.

By the time I was setting up Howdens I'd been in business long enough to know that in addition to the right name, we needed the right symbol to represent the business. We needed to be thinking about design. We needed – to use the jargon – a 'brand identity'.

I knew just the person to talk to – Jeff Kindleysides. Jeff had a business, Checkland Kindleysides, and he'd done some work for me at Magnet, designing our trade logo. For that, for the Magnet logo, I'd known exactly the colours I wanted, if little else: blue, suggesting authority and calm, with yellow to make it stand out, and a little dash of red to suggest urgency. Three colours, in obvious combination – easy. But inevitably this led to all sorts of high-level executive chat about what *exact* shade of yellow and should it be royal blue or navy blue and how much red and it all got very complicated. But then I was at this trade show in Milan with Mike McIlroy – who was the production director for Magnet – and we were wandering around and at this one stand there were a bunch of these very glamorous Italian women in boiler suits. Very Italian. It was the Magneti Marelli stand – they do automotive parts. And the boiler suits were the *exact* colour I was looking for. So I went up to the guy who was running the stand and I said I really like the clothes the women are wearing. And he said, what? This was all in broken English and Italian, of course. I really like their clothes, I said. I didn't know the Italian word for boiler suit. I like their clothes, I repeated. I'd like some of their clothes. Anyway, in the end I thought I'd just about managed to make my intentions clear – I was interested in the clothes, not the women – and the Italian called over one of the women and explained to her what I wanted and she looked a bit shocked and perplexed, but we shook hands and did the deal, there and then. You want it now, he said. The boiler suit? No, no, no, I said. Not now! It could all have got a bit embarrassing. Ah, OK, said the Italian. I'll have it wrapped and sent to you. Do you want it washed, my friend, or do you prefer it as it is?

Anyway, the dry-cleaned Italian boiler suit eventually arrived, and it was exactly the right shade and combination of colours, and Jeff used it as the basis for the colours of the Magnet Trade logo. He did a brilliant job. Jeff is a man who can follow a brief – no matter how unusual the circumstances.

So, in the summer of 1995 I said to Jeff, look, I'm starting this new business, I'm going to call it Howdens, and it needs to look like a heritage business, like it's been around for years. And Jeff just said, fine. No boiler suits involved? No. Leave it with me, he said. And I went off on holiday and by the time I came back he'd done it all – the colours, the logo, *everything*.

It was Jeff who came up with the famous Howdens red cockerel symbol – harking on the Houdan hen, the colour symbolising confidence, and in a style that suggests the stencils used to brand Scandinavian timber. It was also Jeff who suggested we use a cream background to add some warmth to the image and to suggest the colour of sawn timber. Plus a nice plain, utilitarian typeface that looked as though it had been around since the 1930s. The whole thing was absolutely perfect.

The name was certainly a start, but the logo and the typeface allowed me to clearly connect what I was embarking upon with my new venture with my own family history – the Duxbury family history – and everything they had achieved, buying up the old ammo boxes after the war, so that people could make their chicken runs and sheds, dealing direct with builders, a family business with values and principles.

Over the years, Jeff's design skills have been crucial to the development of Howdens – you really cannot underestimate

The Howdens logo

The logo was designed around the brand story... two brothers who started by making chicken sheds...

It felt appropriate to make our logo look like the stencilled mark that quality timber merchants use... of course our mark would be a rooster.

the significance of symbols and signs. You can't underestimate the significance of someone like Jeff. He later went on to design the Lamona brand – our electrical appliances – and then when we got into difficulties at MFI and we sold the public company and we needed a business to protect the Howdens name, Jeff came up with the name Galiform. (La Mona and Galiform are also breeds of hen, by the way: if you're looking for a brand name, if in doubt, use a chicken.)

Did the branding work? Yes. How do I know it worked? Well, here's a story from the Orpington depot, the first week we opened. This young builder comes in with a window which needs a new handle, and we didn't have the handle. The manager says it's not one of our windows, because we've only just opened this week – and the young builder says these immortal words: but my father has been using you for years.

We hadn't just opened a business. We hadn't just created a symbol. We had made history.

A Leap of Faith

Derek's backing. MFI's firepower. A name. A symbol. All I needed now was staff, stock, and some depots.

Because I'd been running Magnet Trade I obviously knew a lot of people in the trade, and indeed a lot of people in Magnet Trade, who I wanted to persuade to come and work with me in my exciting new venture. Somehow I had to persuade these people that Howdens wasn't going to be some flash in the pan, some foolish fly-by-night sort of enterprise. I couldn't be asking people – old friends and colleagues – to give up their security and leave their jobs and join me on a whim. I had to be able to offer them something substantial, something serious – not just a little adventure, but a proper career. Fortunately, MFI at the time were very secure financially and very well respected, so I knew I was going to be able to offer not only the prospect of being in at the start of something new, but also – crucially – a pension and a car. I could offer employees the benefits of being part of a big business while being part of a small start-up business. Also, because Magnet were in the process of merging trade back with retail, I knew that a lot of the people I wanted to recruit – trade people – weren't too keen on staying where they were. I knew I was going to be able to say to them, look, read the runes, wake up and smell the coffee. This is the way Magnet is going, but if you come with me we're going to be able to take everything good that we've learnt together over the past few years and we're going to be able to put it into practice properly at Howdens. We've got the support, we're guaranteed the supply, and given that we've all worked together before, it's all going to be fine.

On paper, it sounded good. On paper, it sounded great. I knew I could make the argument. But it was still going to be a leap of faith. I needed the first person – I needed someone to jump.

That person was Keith Sims. Keith had been Magnet's regional manager for London, recently demoted to working in East Anglia. Keith was and is a brilliant communicator, a man who sincerely believes in the trade. I'd worked with Keith for many years. If Keith came, others would follow. All I had to do was persuade him to come over to Howdens.

So I rang Keith and I said, look, I've got a business proposition for you. OK, he said. I'll tell you what, I said. I'll take you for a curry and explain it to you. Bring the wife.

So we arranged to meet. I said I'd pick him up – and I took the precaution of driving to see him in the company car he'd be getting if he came to work for me. At the time, he was driving around in something like an old Sierra. So I arrive in this brand new Rover, automatic, top of the range, and Keith and his wife Janet get in this lovely car and we go to the restaurant and we have a nice meal and talk about my vision for the business and how Keith would be an essential part of it. And I knew that whatever I was saying to Keith, I was really saying to Janet, because she could have put a stop to it at any moment. Anyway, the conversation went well and Keith and Janet said they'd think about it and I eventually dropped them back home, pulled into the driveway – and just as he was getting out of the car Keith asked what car he'd be driving if he came to work with me at Howdens. I said, you're in it, Keith. This is the car. And I knew that was it. That was the clincher.

With Keith in place, the word soon went out – news sort of seeped under the door. My old Magnet friend and colleague Andy Witts called and said he'd heard that I was starting something new and he might be interested, and we met in the McDonald's in Bristol, and he agreed to come over. I met Steve Taylor, Dale Williams – stalwarts. Stout fellows. We ran an ad in the *Grocer* magazine, of all places, so that everything was above board and legal but no one in our industry would suspect that we were recruiting. And within six weeks of me starting at MFI I had a full complement of staff.

Six weeks: the result of a lifetime spent building good relationships. Because a leap of faith is built on trust.

The Pollen Path

The Navajos tell the story of 'the pollen path'. It's the path through life that is true to the individual, that reflects your own individual interests and passions, that is unique to you. On the pollen path, every leaf and every branch along the path, the ground below, the sky above, *everywhere* looks as if it is covered in pollen. Everything just seems right, lined up, the sun is shining but not too hot – it is a world of possibility.

I believe that if you want to achieve something, if you want to get something done, you need to help people along their way. You need to help them find the pollen path.

That principle certainly applied when I was building our team at Howdens, but it applied throughout our business generally. Seek the true path. Find the best route. Literally.

I remember when our children were young; they used to play with toy trucks, and I would play a game with them. So we've got our toy truck, now what's the quickest way of getting all of these things – let's say, for the sake of argument, a load of kitchen cabinets – from here to over there? I've got lots and lots of trucks – do I put a few kitchen cabinets on each truck, or do I take one truck and completely fill it, and only when it's full do I send it on its journey?

When you put it like that, the answer's obvious. Let's make sure when a truck arrives at our depot that it comes from one place, that it's as full as it can possibly be, that you know when it's coming, that you've already got plenty of stock – so you don't have to worry if there are problems with the delivery – so that everything's perfectly calm and under control.

Logistics? The pollen path.

The pollen path...

The A Team

In a sense, putting together our senior management team, the first depot managers, was the easy part. I rang round, I met people, but I knew that to really get them on board I was going to have to persuade their families that this whole thing was a good idea. Getting a business going is not just about the people you're recruiting and employing – it's also about their families, their partners, everyone they know. Can these people say with pride to the bloke down the pub, or the person they meet at the golf club, or when they play football, or at the gym, or to the other mums and dads at the school gate, that this is what their husband or wife or son or daughter or father or mother is doing?

In August 1995 I decided to hold an away day, a bit of a get-together, and I plumped for Brands Hatch, in Kent, home of the old British Grand Prix, an iconic site, a racetrack – and easily accessible for everyone. Keith Sims lived nearby. Dale Williams. Steve Taylor could get there from Portsmouth. Andy Witts. Chris Youell. I wanted to make life easy for people. (I remember years later, when we had to close some central offices down, I used the same principle – find a new office, I said, close to where you live. And lo and behold, we found our new local offices pretty quickly. Go where people are.)

So we got our little team together, got everyone driving a few cars around the track, which was great fun, and then we all had a meal together, husbands and wives, family members, and it enabled me to say a few words about what I thought this new-fangled Howdens business was all about. Joinery from stock, for trade, from depots throughout the country, supplied from our own warehouses. A local business with big ambitions.

For me, this wasn't just an important moment in the business, this was one of the great moments of my career. Realising that all these people – these families – had put their trust in me, and that I needed to return that trust by doing what I said I was going to do with Howdens.

When you're building a team it's not just about the team. You also need the support of those people who support the team.

Bonfire Night

Here's what I mean about teams.

I remember back in the early 1980s. We were in Leeds. It was Bonfire Night. The 5th of November. We'd been invited to a party at a friend's house. And when we arrived there was a big crowd – families, friends. But no sign of any bonfire. So I thought I'd better get things organized.

I got a few blokes and some older boys together to go and find some logs. And then this little lad came up to me and said that the big boys weren't allowing him to help find the logs. Well, I said, you need to go and get us some sticks. Because we won't be able to get the fire going without some kindling. And off he went.

And then a little girl came and asked if there was anything she could do to help – she was inside with the women, getting the food prepared. Yes, I said. You could go and find me some matches, because the fire won't get going without some matches. And off she went, only to return with some matches – and a bucket with some firelighters. Where'd you get the firelighters? I asked. It was that lady, she said. And it was my wife, Sarah, who'd thought of the firelighters.

You need a team. You need everybody's buy-in. You need to put everybody to work. And then – with any luck – you can rely on everyone to work it out for themselves.

Worthwhile for All Concerned

One of the principles I developed in the early days at Howdens was the idea that our business should be worthwhile for all concerned. That doesn't mean I'm a communist. I don't think we should all be paid the same. It doesn't mean we give our products away. But the business should be worthwhile for all concerned – staff, customers, shareholders, suppliers, the local community, everyone.

It's a principle that can be applied to other areas of life – not just business. The day, the event, the relationship, the marriage – whatever it is. Did you learn something? Did you enjoy it? Was it worthwhile for all concerned?

Making it worthwhile for all concerned doesn't necessarily take a lot. It often requires just a bit of forethought – making things easy, giving people something to look forward to. I think one of the things that depresses people the most is when they have nothing to look forward to. I remember when I was at school, the food was so dreadful, and just once a term we were served soup, but we all looked forward to being served soup. I haven't forgotten that.

Early on at Howdens we developed the idea of having a depot pot – apart from the bonus that individuals received themselves, some money was put aside if a depot had done well, on the condition that the money had to be spent on something the team did together. It could be anything. A trip. Some sort of outing or activity. Something worthwhile for all concerned. Crucially, the staff paid nothing towards it themselves. And it had to be in working hours, in the working week. You can't tell your people that we're going to do this fun thing together this weekend – because that's not a reward, that's an imposition.

Worthwhile for all concerned also means paying people properly – and doing what you said you were going to do. I remember one year we got around to our annual wage award and people said of course we won't be paying that increase this year, Matthew – and I said, of course we will. But we can't afford that, Matthew. Guess what? We can't afford not to.

Want to make your business a success? Make it worthwhile for all concerned.

Ritzy Depots

The team were in place. Everyone was on board. Now we just needed some products, and some depots.

At that time, MFI had a brilliant property director, a man named Jim McManus. He was absolutely brilliant, Jim, just a lovely man – a brilliant raconteur, self-deprecating, modest, charming. The story goes that his career began when he walked into his local MFI in Catford one day and asked if they had a job, and he was taken on immediately as a warehouseman. And from there he gradually worked his way up. By the time Derek Hunt took over, Jim had become an area controller – a senior sales manager – and Derek took a liking to him and decided he'd make a good property director for the whole company. That's what Derek was like – he went with his gut instinct. He liked Jim and thought he'd do a good job, and that was enough. But I don't know anything about property, said Jim. That's all right, said Derek. I'll teach you. I just need someone I can trust.

His trust was well-placed.

Jim was a great connector – above all, he knew how to find the right people. It was Jim who found us Alan 'Ritzy' Davies.

Ritzy was a legend. He was something else, Ritzy – he was like a little ferret, like something out of a children's book. He wore these velvet suits and he had a gold watch chain and he smoked big cigars and he frequented all these fancy restaurants and bars – but he was always sniffing out property deals. Jim knew Ritzy – and Ritzy knew property.

So Ritzy came in to see us and we told him we needed some depots. This was April 1995. And we needed the depots up and running by October. Fine. Leave it with me, says Ritzy. I'll be back in a week.

And right enough he was back in a week, but the sites he'd found were too expensive.

No problem, says Ritzy, give me another week. And let me just check again – you want each of these depots to be around 10,000 square feet, with racks and a trade counter, yeah? That's right, Ritzy, that's what we're after.

And that was it. That was enough. Ritzy found us our first fourteen depots. I used to go round with him in his car. He just had a nose for it. He could sniff them out.

They were nothing special, the depots. We didn't need them all the same shape and size. Most of them didn't even have hot running water. All we needed was a place to accommodate all our stock, where we could stick in a Cona coffee machine and a TV and open up for business. That was it.

At the time, no one was doing it like that. People always tend to make things far too complicated. All the depots have to look the same, or they have to be on similar sites. They have to be like this or that. And then you'll need this sort of racking in all of them, this sort of counter. And these sorts of facilities. And then you'll need uniforms. It just goes on and on, and it's all money out of your pocket. All we wanted were depots where everything was in stock. That was it.

The first depot was in Orpington. I knew exactly where I wanted the first depot. I'd only left Magnet six months previously and I knew they had a depot there and I thought, fine, let's put our depot right next door. Let's take them on directly. Nelson: engage the enemy more closely.

Of course, we didn't tell anyone about it. It was all hush hush and undercover, but then one day BT came along to put the telephone line in and told them Howdens Joinery were coming in – and so our cover was blown. Fortunately we were moving so fast it didn't really matter.

There were all the usual problems. You couldn't run a forklift under the door – well, let's just get a smaller forklift. Don't get it right. Get it done. Let's just get it open. What you were doing was trusting people and learning as you went. If we'd decided we had to have a perfect layout with perfect plans and drawings it would never have happened.

MFI had been incredibly helpful. But then they decided they wanted a grand opening. And their idea of a grand opening was chorus girls, leaflet drops to local builders' homes. A whole lot of razzamatazz. And I just said no. I had to put my foot down. I said this is not what we're about. I said builders are decent family people. They don't need glamour girls. And they don't want to see us wasting money on a lot of old nonsense.

Sometimes you don't need it ritzy. But you will always need a Ritzy.

Old Canals and Burger Vans

When it came to selecting the sites for the depots it was clear that we were going to choose out-of-town sites, which were going to be much cheaper per square foot than retail space in busy town centres. But there were certain other rather specific criteria that applied.

As I explained to Ritzy, the sites had to be low-cost, they had to be able to take a small trade counter, be mostly warehouse, be around 10,000 square feet, at a cost of about £5.50 per square foot, and be capable of carrying about £150,000 of stock.

Oh, and they all had to be close to canals and burger vans. Why?

It was partly me harking back to my days in the timber yard in Huddersfield, down by the canal. This was where manufacturing businesses in the UK began – around the canals and rivers. Around the canals and rivers of the UK you still tend to have excellent transport links – because they were once the main sites of industry. History runs deep not only in our minds, but in the landscape. Old canals are the Silk Roads of England.

I also knew that we needed to be sited near the best burger vans. I knew from years of driving round the country working for Magnet that if you find a good roadside burger van, you're always going to find your local builders, fuelling up between jobs. I reckoned if we could source our sites near the best burger vans, then the builder would be able to grab his breakfast, pick up his materials for the day in our depot and go and get on with the job. Because what does every builder want? They want to get the job done quickly, to the customer's satisfaction, get paid and move on to the next job.

When we were looking for suitable sites, we ate a hell of a lot of burgers – and a lot of bacon baps and sausage sandwiches. We drank a lot of tea. It was worth it.

Make the work easy for yourself and others: seek out the canals and the burger vans. Understand the past and the present – they will guide you to your future.

The Jigsaw Without the Box

When I think back now to the beginning of Howdens I realise that I had plenty of pieces to work with. All I really did was put the jigsaw together – though without the picture on the box to guide me.

That's one way of thinking about business.

Ask and Ye Shall Receive

April–October 1995: the jigsaw was coming together. This was the period of creation. This was our genesis moment. The brand was developed, the people and the places had been chosen. Now we needed some product.

The first thing I did was go looking for doors. My first stop was John Carr Joinery in Doncaster – a top-class family business, specialising in doors and stairs and stair parts. I was shown in, welcomed, I explained to them what we were planning to do at Howdens and how things would work, and they quoted me a very reasonable commercial price. That'd be great, I said. Deal. Very good, Matthew, where do you want us to send the pro forma invoice? Oh, I said. No. I need it done on credit terms. We're so sorry, they said, we can't offer you credit terms – it's going to have to be cash before delivery. Well, I said, I can't do that. And we can't do you credit, they said. But actually we're part of the MFI group, I said. Ah. Well, that changed everything. No problem, they said. Credit terms it is. And so we got our doors.

Another simple lesson: you can try and do it yourself, but sometimes, without some help and some backing, you might never get started.

It was the same story in the early days of Howdens, again and again. I remember putting our first catalogue together. I met someone called Rob Hunt, who worked for MFI. We met at the Old Swan Hotel on a winter's day and he helped me put together some things from MFI that might work as part of our trade range, which was extremely helpful – but it all looked wrong in the catalogue. It looked too retail, it wasn't right.

So over the weekend I chopped the catalogue up and stuck it on some white paper in a rough and ready fashion and then I took it to the catalogue people at MFI on the Monday and showed them how it needed to look. And they just took it and did it. And the catalogue was done.

I was lucky. I needed I help. I asked for help. I received the help.

On another occasion, when we started to fit out the depots, I explained to Andy Fisk, who was in charge of the fit-outs, that we had a budget of about £4,000 per depot. He laughed. He said the minimum he could do a depot for was about £40,000. We just can't do it for £4,000, said Andy. Well, how about if we just hammer some MDF against a wall and get our local managers to ask local builders to put a couple of kitchens together for our displays, I said. OK, said Andy. No problem.

Another example – a crucial example. When I was at Magnet we'd sold something called a Module 500, which was a robust plain white kitchen, with an aluminium strip underneath the door. It was originally designed for councils. It was indestructible. It was the kitchen you'd have in schools, in doctor's surgeries, everywhere. It wasn't particularly pretty but it was hygienic, it was easy to fit, and above all it didn't break. And unless you've got that sort of thing in your catalogue you're not really running a trade business. The Module 500 was your workhorse kitchen. Standard issue, not expensive – the Module 500 was your basic bread and butter.

So when I started Howdens I knew we needed our Module 500. There's no way we can do it, I was told. The factory can't do it. So I went to see the person who ran the factory – he was called Bob Wilson – and I said, look, Bob, I need a Module 500-type unit, with the aluminium strips. We can't get the strips, he said. Well, if I could get the strips, I said, could you do it? Of course, he said.

So I called a man I knew, my old friend John Stephenson, of Stephenson's hardware – the man who was always and already prepared. If John could rustle up a Mercedes-Benz fire engine at the drop of a hat, I was pretty sure he was capable of getting us some aluminium strips. And I was right. Aluminium strips, Matthew? Certainly, no problem. How many do you want?

Problem solved.

I needed help. I asked for help. I received the help.

One more final example – again, a crucial example. This one was really make or break. Basically, if you're doing trade kitchens you need to provide rigid cabinets. You can't be mucking around with flat-pack. Flat-pack is a nightmare. Everyone knows that. Flat-pack is a complete waste of time. Your builder does not want to spend hours fiddling around with an Allen key trying to put some fiddly thing together. A builder wants to pick up some rigid cabinets, get them on site, get them in place, and then they're gone on to their next job. So if you're running a trade business, flat-pack is no good. There's always something going wrong with flat-pack.

And of course just as we were about to get up and running with Howdens we were told that MFI were going to be shutting their Runcorn factory and so they could no longer do rigid – our kitchens would all have to be flat-pack.

No.

Just no.

I knew that flat-pack was no good. If Howdens was going to have to be flat-pack, Howdens was not going to happen.

So I rang Derek Hunt and told him that if we couldn't do rigid, we couldn't do it. A lot of people under those circumstances might have said, well, fine, that's the situation, we'll just have to do our best to sell flat-pack. But by speaking up, by asking for help, we kept with rigid construction. And we kept Runcorn open. It's still running today.

I needed I help. I asked for help. I received the help.

I was lucky? Maybe. I was pushy? Probably. I was determined? Certainly.

Stick to Your Principles

Sticking to your principles is important. As long as you know what your principles are.

I remember being reminded of a remark by Clayton Christensen, who was a professor at Harvard Business School: 'It's easier to hold to your principles 100 per cent of the time than it is to hold to them 98 per cent of the time.'

Easier? Maybe. Sensible, for sure.

State Your Purpose

Your principles are one thing, your purpose is another.

Our purpose at Howdens was perfectly simple. I can recite it now from memory, our purpose, as it came to me at the time, in the very early days:

To provide from local stock nationwide the small builders' routine joinery and kitchen requirements, at the best local price, and with a no callback quality guarantee.

When it comes down to it, businesses solve problems. At Howdens we set out to solve problems for small builders doing joinery and kitchens.

If you can understand the problem you're setting out to solve, then you can begin to work out what your business has to do, how it has to act, what it looks like, feels like – everything. It's a form of reverse engineering. Form follows function.

If we wanted to serve local builders effectively, we needed to fit into their local area, their society. We needed to understand and associate with them, we needed to be from them and among them. We needed to understand that builders are basically business people – thoroughly decent, hard-working businessmen and women who don't get paid until a job is done and done right, and who need to keep getting it right, time and time again, in order for them to be able to thrive and prosper in their local communities. Being a builder is a bloody difficult job.

If you really understand and appreciate that – if you really understand and appreciate your customers and their problems – everything else follows.

For us, it meant that we had to meet certain basic standards and requirements: our kitchens needed to be easy to fit; they had to be sturdy and robust; they had to be available locally and when required; their parts had to be swapped easily and efficiently; we needed to be able to offer good credit terms and help provide a good margin to builders working with narrow margins and on deferred payments; and we had to create a

comfortable trade environment, in which our staff were able to respond to local needs and build long-term relationships of trust.

Understanding all of that necessarily had consequences for how we built the business. It meant we had to offer the best prices, the best quality and always have stock available – which meant having suppliers who shared our philosophy and approach. It meant having motivated and well-paid staff. It meant having low central overheads, because tradesmen and builders don't care about big central offices in London.

State your purpose, solve a problem – and then you might have a business.

Factories and Societies

Getting the initial problems with the Runcorn factory sorted was absolutely crucial – because factories are the heart and soul of a business like Howdens. Having started out in the timber yards, I know what it's like working in a factory: it's hard work.

A well-run yard or a factory is like a society in miniature. Everyone gets to know the people they're working with – they work together, they eat together. It's a community. We currently have about 1,200 staff working at our factory at Howden and about 450 in Runcorn. These places are like small villages or towns.

I've always believed that it's a mistake to try and buy your goods cheaper from abroad just because you can. I've done it. We've all done it. But I think fundamentally it's wrong. It's a mistake – for purely practical reasons. If I know exactly where something is made and I can go there right now, or I can ring the manager down the road and he can get there right now, then whatever the problem is, it's going to be fine. But if a product is being manufactured a thousand miles away, or two thousand miles away, and I have no means of communicating clearly and directly and quickly with the manufacturer, eventually I am going to run into serious problems.

Our UK factories are the backbone of the business. The Runcorn factory was built by Schreiber, the German furniture company, to German furniture company standards. It's just a superb facility. When it was built in the mid-1970s it was the largest single-span building in the country, and it's pretty impressive even today.

In Howden, meanwhile, we are lucky enough to be working out of the old Hygena factory, which was originally built by Malcolm Healey to supply MFI, before he sold the business to them. It's another superb facility.

We may now have a London office, but the factories, the depots – these are the places where our business is based. If I had to pick my all-time favourite among all our various sites I would have to say that I'm particularly fond of our old Keighley depot, which is close to the old Keighley Magnet depot, which is where I spent so much time when I was at Magnet, learning the trade. Even now, more than forty years on, when I'm in Keighley I still recognise people from all those years ago – and am recognised by them. Going to Keighley feels like going home. It's quite a thing. I've always loved Keighley. It's a tough, proud, no-nonsense sort of a town. I always think if you can trade in Keighley, you can trade anywhere. I have. We have.

We're big. But we're local. Which is how it should be.

A (Very Short)
History of British Kitchens

Name, brand, staff, depots, products, production facilities, and a purpose: we were underway. But in order to properly understand what we went on to do at Howdens – exactly what we achieved – you probably need to understand a little bit about the history of the British kitchen. This is my version of Walt Disney's famous Carousel of Progress – that animatronic show at Disney World in Florida, which takes you through the history of the twentieth century via the life of a typical American family – Uncle Walt's favourite attraction, apparently. Buckle up.

I'll take my own family as an example. Our family kitchen when I was a child – I'm talking about the 1950s here – would have been a pretty typical British kitchen of its time. It consisted of a few dark blue-painted cabinets, made out of plywood, with little bent aluminium handles on the front and corrugated paper and old wallpaper inside for lining, a kitchen table pushed up against the wall, a top-loading washing machine on the tiled floor, a tap into the sink with a bit of old hosepipe attached for various plumbing and connection purposes, a mangle that was ceremoniously hauled up over the sink on washing day, plus a hole cut in the old wooden work surface for the bin. And that was it. No frills, no gadgets.

(My grandfather's kitchen, I should say – this was my grandfather Ingle – was rather exceptional. He had a big old table, with an old black range, and he'd built a kennel in the corner, like a little cupboard with a door, for his dog Twiddles.

Real life in the Kitchen

The kitchen is a place to cook, to eat, to work. It's a study, a surgery, a vets, a place to laugh, to cry, to chat... it is the heart of the home.

He was a very particular man, my grandfather – he'd been educated in Germany. He did everything properly. His lawn, for example, was absolutely flat and perfectly free-draining. I've never seen anything quite like it. Years later, someone was renting his house and I was there sorting out a few things and I discovered an air-raid shelter hidden away, fully equipped and ready to use, with beds and tinned food, the works. You could have lived in his air-raid shelter for months, if not years.)

Kitchens back in the 1950s were still functional spaces, containing just the bare essentials. No one would have dreamt of relaxing or socialising in their kitchen: the front room, the parlour or the drawing room served as the centre of the household, where the family would gather round the fire or wireless for entertainment. Also you have to remember that after the Second World War, times were still pretty hard. There was little enough of anything to go round; wartime rationing continued well on into the 1950s. Every last scrap of wood and metal had been salvaged to support the war effort, fresh seasonal food had to be bought in most days, a few tinned goods were kept in a cupboard or a larder, refrigeration was uncommon and a home washing machine unimaginable.

But big changes – social, political and technological changes – soon had an impact on how kitchens were designed and used. Women became an integral and irreplaceable part of the workforce – which meant that where once women might have been expected to spend many hours in the kitchen baking, cooking, washing and cleaning, there was now a demand for labour-saving devices. Heat-resistant laminates and stainless steel cabinets, man-made fabrics and all kinds of plastics started to become widely available. Formica – colourful, cheap and cheerful – became ubiquitous. Under-counter and over-counter cupboards and shelves became de rigeur. Fridges became commonplace, gadgets became must-haves, and eventually there were the built-in fridges, the dishwashers, the twin ovens, the microwaves, the extractor hoods and then the pine tables and plants and rugs and goodness knows what else, inspired by Terence Conran and his vision of continental living. By the 1980s and 1990s the kitchen had become a consumer good, a fashion statement – something you could design to suit your particular needs. The kitchen was no longer just a site of food preparation. It had become a statement about who you were.

Which is where Howdens came in.

Premium

Here's a quick cautionary kitchen tale – and a recommendation, in case you're thinking of having a kitchen fitted anytime soon.

Some years ago we bought a little cottage which had a Smallbone kitchen installed – Smallbone make these bespoke, hand-crafted kitchens. They're the best of the best. Top of the range. Pure luxury. They're the Porsche of kitchens. This kitchen was solid oak, with African slate worktops, there were drawers within cupboards within drawers, it was like a Chinese puzzle box, this kitchen. You name it, it had it. It was magnificent. It was beyond bespoke. We were very lucky. It was like a work of art. The trouble was, they'd tried to cram too much in – the whole thing was too much. It was beautiful but impractical.

At Howdens what we set out to do was the opposite – to provide beautiful, practical, affordable kitchens, excellent ordinary kitchens, sold at a good price to builders, plus joinery, handles, doors. That was our model. But over the years even we were tempted towards luxury and expense – and once you go there, you're in trouble. It causes more problems than it's worth – and it's entirely unnecessary.

What happened was that people started buying bigger and bigger kitchens from us, because we were always in stock and because they could customise it. I remember once I was talking to a friend's wife about her kitchen – which was really a magnificent kitchen, absolutely vast, like something out of a stately home. Where did you get this? I asked. It's one of yours, Matthew, she said. And even I was impressed. Their builder had tweaked it with various features, including gold-plated handles. It looked like a bespoke kitchen. It was really spectacular.

So, the temptation is to drift towards luxe, giant and bespoke. The temptation if you're running a Howdens depot is that a designer comes to you and says they've got a builder looking for a £50,000 kitchen, which is a hell of a lot of money for a kitchen, so can we give them an extra 5 per cent discount. Well of course we could, but that would mean we couldn't give the same discount to a builder looking for a £5,000 or £10,000 kitchen. We often had the same thing in the early days of the business, where we would get reps selling to new builds where they would demand specials or discounts because of the size of the order. You start to take that on, you start to do that, and your business can soon become determined by those large influential orders. You become an entirely different sort of operation. It's Skipton Market Rules: do what you do and nothing else.

Now that doesn't mean that you don't change or alter your offering to suit the market. A man named Jeremy Cecil-Wright taught me many years ago that there are basically three categories of product: there's good, there's better, and there's the best. Even you, Matthew, he'd say, can remember that. Three – and three only – categories of product. Well, he was almost right. Because there's also budget – which is as cheap as you can get – and there's premium. And premium turns out to be a very interesting place to be. Premium is not the best, but it's better than good. In marketing terms premium is like John Lewis, or the BMW Alpina, which is not a 7 series, but it's a nice technical car for those who appreciate a nice technical car but who can't afford a 7 series. In kitchen terms, premium is high gloss rather than solid oak. Premium is better than good.

In any business, you always need a good range – from budget to premium, or somewhere in between. And in the kitchen business, always remember that a good joiner or fitter can make good look better and the better look the best.

Do What You Say You're Going to Do

So we opened our first fourteen Howdens depots in late September 1995 with half a dozen kitchen ranges.

Each depot had advertised locally, but the early days were quiet – too quiet. I was on the phone constantly, asking questions, seeing what we could do to get things going. It was pretty nerve-wracking. The volume of sales was just too low. There was a sense that we hadn't got off to the right start – and by the time it got to Christmas I began to wonder how many of our new colleagues would be returning in the new year. Things were that bad. We'd failed to attract enough customers – and now it looked like we might lose our staff.

But they stuck with us.

Why?

Because we stuck with them. I wasn't going to let them down – and they didn't let me down. We did what we said we were going to do. It's crucial. If you don't, you are doomed.

A year previously, back at Magnet, they'd run a winter sale and had come up with a very daring – a very aggressive – bonus plan which meant that staff could potentially earn in excess of around £10,000 in just six weeks if the sale went well. This was serious money. This was brand new car or deposit on a house type money. And it wasn't just for managers – it was for all staff. It was an absolute bonanza. Not surprisingly, the sale had gone rather well. In fact, it went so well that it was extended – with the promise of even bigger payouts for staff. It turned into the biggest Magnet sale of all time.

Everything was looking good for them.

Until, that is, Magnet's new owners looked at the figures and just said no, we're not paying. And they pulled the plug on it.

It was an extraordinary error of judgement, in all sorts of ways. They had broken the Golden Rule. They did not do what they said they were going to do. There were all these people in the Magnet depots and showrooms – ordinary, decent working people – who had put in the extra hours to ensure the success of the sale and who had been promised these big payouts and then they were told they were getting nothing. It was awful. There was uproar. It was an absolute disaster.

For me, it was a massive opportunity.

I remember I'd been on holiday after Christmas and I was sitting waiting for our baggage at Gatwick Airport and I picked up a paper and there was a headline, something along the lines of 'Magnet cancels bonus plan'. And in that instant I knew that if I ever had a chance of recruiting the staff I needed for my new venture, this was it.

I seized the opportunity. I started getting calls from disgruntled Magnet employees who wanted to come and work for me on my new project. It was like a switch had been flipped, or someone had turned on a tap. We recruited about twenty-eight people for our depots, all from Magnet. In an instant, I had everyone I needed.

I brought them on board, and I stuck by them – and a year later, after our shaky start, we started to get the sales. By the end of our first year's trading, by the end of 1996, our minimum staff in each depot had increased from two to five and our targets were being exceeded. We were on our way.

At the beginning of 1995 Howdens did not exist. It was just a twinkle in my eye. There was no name, there was no product, no buildings, no staff.

Five years later, we had 100 depots.

By the early 2000s our sales exceeded £100 million.

Within twenty years we were employing over 8,000 staff, in 650 locations, with 400,000 accounts.

And all of that is largely because we did what we said we were going to do.

No fairy stories. No flim flam. And if you say you're going to do it, you do it – bonuses included.

Every Cat in the Garden

Over the years I was lucky enough to learn a lot of lessons, directly and indirectly, from a lot of very clever people – people much cleverer than me. And one of the things I noticed was that they would often have these little sayings or remarks that they liked to repeat, and which would stick in my mind – and which I eventually made my own and which became a part of my lexicon and a part of the lore and language of Howdens.

Like: you can't chase every cat in the garden.

That's a classic.

The phrase originated with Jeremy Cecil-Wright. Jeremy is another one of those people who might rightfully claim to having taught me everything I know. He worked for A. T. Kearney, the management consultants. I was never a big fan of management consultants, but Jeremy was different. Jeremy was a genius when it came to pointing out the obvious. He knew what was what and who was who and when to call a spade a spade. And he had these little phrases, like, you can't chase every cat in the garden.

So, let's say you decide you're going to start a business selling kitchens and joinery – who could you sell to, Matthew? Builders who are doing new builds, who are building new homes? Fine. Anyone else? People doing repairs and maintenance? Fine. Anyone else? No, that's probably about it. So, that's your market. And who's currently supplying them? If you're running a repairs and maintenance business or you're a small builder you're probably going to be buying from Wickes or B&Q or Jewson. So, if you are setting up your kitchen and joinery business you now know your market and your competitors. In a few quick logical steps, with a simple exercise of the little grey cells, with a few quick strokes of the pen, you can see exactly what sort of business you're in.

And once you've identified your market and your competitors you can then be absolutely clear about your own business. You mustn't be tempted to run after every opportunity. You might be supplying some builders working on new builds, but does that mean you want to start supplying the big developers, with their central buying systems and their architects, with this demand and that requirement? No. You have to be absolutely clear. It goes back to Skipton Market

You can't catch every cat in the garden.

Rules. If you're selling oranges you're selling oranges: they might be big ones, they might be small ones, they might be pretty ones wrapped in tissue paper, but they're still oranges. Occasionally at Christmas you might sell satsumas. But fundamentally you are an orange-seller. You are not selling cheese. And why?

Because you can't chase every cat in the garden.

That was Jeremy's point. Get good at something. Be grateful you're good at something. And do that. Don't do lots of other things: just do that.

I remember I first met Jeremy when things were going wrong at Magnet and the bank insisted on us getting in some consultants. We worked our way through quite a few. But I stuck with Jeremy, and Jeremy stuck with me. Because you can't chase every cat in the garden.

Awareness, Specification, Availability

Jeremy Cecil-Wright not only taught me about the importance of identifying your core business, he also taught me about the importance of understanding market share, and about customers, and about stock. Jeremy always made it simple. If you're a trade business, Matthew, he would say, you need to be in stock, isn't that right? Yes. So the only question is, how much stock do you need? Well, Matthew, you're going need at least two of everything, aren't you. Always. Simple. And when it comes to customers, guess what kind of customers you're going to need? You're going to need some big customers, and you're going to need a lot of small customers. Again, simple.

Then when it comes to market share, Jeremy would say, it's all about awareness, specification and availability. If you want to calculate your market share it looks something like this:

Awareness x Specification x Availability = Market Share

If you take the car market as an example: how big is the car market? It's so much. And your share of that so much is going to come down to awareness, specification and availability.

First, awareness. People have to know that you're selling cars. Unless they know that you're selling cars they're not going to be buying a car from you. It's obvious. It's like winking at a pretty girl in the dark. You can wink all you like – she is not going to be able to see you winking in the dark.

Second, specification. Specification relates to two things: range and quality. You need to have the right range, and you need to have the right quality – which doesn't mean you need the biggest range, or the best quality. You just need the right range and the appropriate quality for what your customer wants. So, if someone decides they want a four-wheel-drive car and you're only selling two-wheel-drives, they're not going to be buying a car from you, because you've ruled yourself out of the four-wheel-drive market. Which is fine. But if everyone is wanting four-wheel-drives, you're going to be in trouble. So your range is important. You need to stock what people want. And when it comes to quality, you also need to know what your customers want. Let's say your son or your daughter is learning to drive and you're thinking of buying a car. All you are going to want is a car that can get them into town and back. If I'm running a car showroom and my market is people who need a little run-around, I need to stock the appropriate cars: it's no good me stocking Range Rovers.

Third, availability. Let's assume that people know you're selling cars, and your cars are the right specification. The third and final question is very simple – is it in stock? Yes or no?

Let's say you're shopping for a Rolls-Royce. You know where to find the Rolls-Royce. And the specification is not a problem – you can have whatever you want. Gold and black with pink upholstery? No problem, sir. But is it available? Well, yes, but it'll take six months. And it'll cost twice what you thought. Oh. It has to be available when people want it – and at the price they can afford.

So, awareness, specification, availability. Jeremy Cecil-Wright knew how to put it simply.

Have they heard of you? Yes or no?

Have you got what they want? Yes or no?

Is it available? Yes or no?

And can they afford it? Yes or no?

And that's it.

That's all you need to work out.

Which sounds simple – because it is. But simple is not easy.

The Hamilton Effect

I discovered at Howdens that if you actually apply these sorts of simple principles and lessons – if you have the courage to actually apply them and not just talk about them – then truly great things can happen. And when great things happen it is remarkable. It seems hard to believe. It looks like magic.

Think about someone like Lewis Hamilton. There's something uncanny about them. For a moment in time, they're simply the best. They're unbeatable.

For a moment in time, in some places, in some fields of endeavour, some people, some ideas, some things are just extraordinary. We've been very lucky to have had that at Howdens.

Of course it doesn't last forever, and I can't pretend to know exactly what the exact combination of parts is when everything does come together: it's clearly something to do with total commitment, plus incredible luck, plus opportunity, and a sudden flourishing of talent combined with hard-won experience and long-crafted skills. It's a combination of all those things and more.

But what I do know is that when you're in it, when you're a part of it, there is nothing quite like it. It's like hydraulics – you get lifted up out of the common herd and for moment in time it seems like you can do nothing wrong. It's the Hamilton effect.

It's there – it's magnificent – and then it's gone. It's a mystery.

Marzipan Layers

Among other things, I was determined that at Howdens we would avoid the mistakes that had been made at Magnet. One of the things I was determined to do was to avoid a lot of management hierarchies. I was determined that the business should not offer a lot of opportunities for the corporate mountaineer – there would be no great peaks to ascend. I wanted a nice flat structure. I wanted to provide good jobs for smart, hard-working local people around the country – that was it. I didn't want some big head office somewhere packed with corporate types making all the decisions and everyone having to refer constantly to them.

That meant avoiding having too many management marzipan layers. Now, don't get me wrong – marzipan is OK. But you don't want too much – just enough. The last thing you need in business is lots of marzipan layers – middle managers endlessly looking for problems to solve.

A lot of people in middle management – a bit like consultants and bankers and other establishment figures – like to have their answers ready-made and then go and find the problem to fit the answer. Or they like to dream up ideas and notions that are never really going to work. Like, because we're selling kitchens, Matthew, how about we start selling food?

No.

Avoid the marzipan.

The Bonus

In order to achieve that flat structure, in order to avoid all the marzipan layers, my idea at Howdens was that our local managers should basically run the show. They would be responsible for their own stock, for recruiting and hiring local staff, for managing their accounts, for doing their own marketing, for laying out the warehouse – for everything. And in return they would receive incentives based on their local profits.

At Howdens, the depot manager is effectively the MD of his or her local business – equipped and enabled to make their own decisions to suit their own local market. It's a form of what you might call decentralised command. Levels of discount offered to builders should be decided locally, the exact items of stock should be decided locally, opening hours, time off, whatever – it's all down to the local team.

And because the depot is like a small business in its own right my strong feeling is that the profit it generates should be shared out equitably among those who work there. It took me a while to work out exactly how to do it – but luckily, once again, I had the example of others to learn from.

When I was at Magnet I had visited a company called Lapeyre in France – they were our French equivalent, a business which produced kitchens, doors, windows. They were a good solid joinery business. When we visited them – when we were thinking about the management buyout – I remember speaking to their Chief Executive about their bonus scheme. The issue he had was that the people working in their depots could end up earning quite a decent salary and then suddenly lose all interest. They might be earning £50,000 or £100,000, for example, and so why would they bother working hard to earn any more? What Lapeyre did was to introduce a bonus scheme for everyone – not just senior staff.

At Howdens I knew that in order to establish ourselves we needed as few as staff as possible, working as hard as possible, working together, with everyone properly rewarded. So we developed a Lapeyre-style bonus model in which the manager would receive 5 per cent of the local profit margin, minus any stock loss, and their staff would receive another 5 per cent of the local gross margin, divided by the number of staff. A completely simple system in which everyone is motivated, and everyone is rewarded. Our staff are responsible for the business – and they're rewarded for being responsible for the business.

Why other people don't use this sort of system I don't know. Of course you need to provide your people with a decent basic package – a salary, a pension, etc. But a business depends on making money, and because it's your local staff who drive the profitability of the business it's them who should be incentivised and rewarded accordingly. It's no good having the bosses creaming off all the benefits – in the end it just doesn't work for the business.

The way it works for us is like this. Every month we produce a profit and loss account for every single depot. It's important that it's absolutely accurate. Chris Youell always made sure our figures were crisp and clear. That's essential. You need the right figures, and you need them fast. So, say you've sold £100,000, at a 50 per cent gross margin, and you've got costs of £40,000 – you've made £10,000. So you'll get a reward on that – 5 per cent. So that's £500 extra to you. Which is not to be sniffed at. But as the Howdens business has developed there are of course many instances where there are depots selling as much as, say, £3 million a year, on a gross margin of 60 per cent, which is £1.8 million, minus costs, which might mean you're making a profit of in excess of a million pounds a year, which at 5 per cent amounts to £50,000 for the depot manager, plus another £50,000 to staff. Which is a very tidy sum indeed. And there's no threshold – it's not one of those awful systems where if you did well last year and you made so much bonus, you can't make the same amount this year. So everyone's a winner.

The only thing you have to avoid if you're a depot manager is losing stock, which comes off your bonus. You cannot lose stock. When I retired a couple of years ago, when we had a turnover of over a billion, I think in that year we lost about £400,000 of stock – which is nothing. In most businesses you could easily be losing stock at a rate of 3–4 per cent – at which point you're losing millions of pounds a year.

This sort of scheme has multiple advantages. It reminds people in senior management positions in your organisation that the money doesn't just roll in – it is generated by the local men and women who are there every day doing the actual work. It's also a good way of motivating staff, encouraging them to work as a team. It means we tend not to have more staff than we need, because local depot managers and teams don't want their bonus shared out equally among too many. And it creates a kind of perpetual motion within the business – you don't need to worry too much about other complex incentive schemes. It just works.

It took me until 1996 to work out the bonus scheme. But once we'd worked it out, we'd worked it out. It's still running today.

Basic Human Decency

Let's be honest, all of this just comes down to treating people right.

A lot of businesses don't seem to want ordinary decent people to work for them – and don't treat them in an ordinary decent fashion. I've never understood that.

Most people want to live where they live, be respected for who they are, earn enough money to be able to support themselves and their families. And that's it. They don't want to be zillionaires. All they're asking for is a little bit of respect, to be treated right when they're at work, and to be rewarded when they do a good job. They don't want someone standing over them, telling them what to do. They don't want to be treated like idiots. They want to be able to go to work, get on with it and enjoy it. It's not that complicated.

Alas, a lot of people don't get that opportunity. And a lot of people miss out entirely. Let's say something goes wrong in your life. You get sick, you get injured, you have a difficult family life. You have a tough upbringing. You don't excel at school. You make a few mistakes. You have to take time out to look after your family. Does that make you a bad person? No, of course not. Does it mean you're no good as an employee? No, of course not. Does it mean you can't add up? No, of course not. Does it mean you can't be a productive and useful member of society? No, of course not.

From the very start with Howdens, my view was that we could do a lot with ordinary decent people who deserved a chance at doing a good honest job for good honest pay, and who deserved to be treated with respect. I know that it's hardly an original and startling philosophy – again, it's just basic human decency – but it meant that I always tried to focus on what people could do rather than what they couldn't. What's the point of trying to get people to do what they can't do? Everyone has things they're not good at. If you're not good at X, fine. You might be good at Y. In which case, guess what, we're not going to make you do X, we're going to get you doing Y. We'll focus on what you're good at. The crucial question for me, when it came to employing people at Howdens, was this: are you a decent person who gets on OK with people and who people want to buy from? In which case, we might be interested.

And again, it's paid off. Over the years, we have appeared in many of those annual surveys and reports conducted by newspapers and magazines and trade bodies about the UK's best companies to work for. It turns out that, year in, year out, we are one of the UK's best companies to work for. These sorts of tables and rankings are based on anonymous employee engagement surveys, which are designed to allow employees to comment on all the various facets of their working environment, all the way from the top leadership to their own managers and teams.

We employ good people – so we're a good company to work for. It's a virtuous circle – and there's also a trickle-down effect. At Howdens we were engaging with our local communities before the term 'corporate social responsibility' became something fashionable that companies were expected to do. We were engaging with local communities because we're a part of local communities. Over the years I'm proud to say that we have not only donated millions of pounds to charities but have planned and supplied and fitted hundreds of kitchens in community centres, village halls, churches and care homes throughout the country – in particular through our support for the Leonard Cheshire charity, which supports individuals with disabilities to be able to live and work independently.

These days people talk about their employee value proposition. The Howdens employee value proposition – though I would never have called it that – is pretty simple. We value and respect our people, whoever they are, wherever they are, whatever they do, and we do everything in our power to look after them in and out of the workplace, and we reward them well for their time, energy and skills. And that's it. Basic human decency.

Fix the Leak in the Roof

A lot of companies these days like to talk about being investors in people. Which is fine. But to be clear – it is just talk. Anyone can talk about investing in people. It's another thing to *actually* invest in them. Investing in people means listening to them and taking them seriously. It's no good talking about investing in people – you have to actually invest in them.

So, let's say there's a young person in one of our depots or in the factory and there's a leak in the roof. Would you want your son or your daughter to be working somewhere where there's a leak in the roof? No, of course not. So you have to stop the leaks in the roof. You have to demonstrate that you are investing in your people. Basic things. Basic courtesies. People will often say they can't afford it – the truth is, you can't afford not to do it. Fix the leak in the roof.

Or let's just imagine – purely hypothetically – that there's a bloke in a depot who's a difficult old so-and-so, but an absolutely excellent depot manager. One of the best. He does so well you make him an area manager, but then he decides he doesn't like it. He wants to go back to running his own little depot. Do you take the opportunity to get rid of him, because he's a difficult old so-and-so? No, of course you don't. You bring him back into the depot, because you are investing in people. He's learnt a valuable lesson, you've learnt a valuable lesson. Crack on. Get over it. Get on with it.

You're not just talking about it, you're doing it.

Those Back of the Diary Figures

Now, let me be clear: in the end, nothing counts in business except making money. The best way we can take care of our people is by staying in business. That's the rule.

Remember Skipton Market Rules: if you're a market trader you're up early in the morning, off to the wholesalers, you set up your market stall, come rain or shine, and you have to be off the street by 5 p.m. And that's your moment of reckoning. Every day. Have you got more money at the end of the day than you had at the start of the day? Yes or no?

Middle management tend to shy away from this basic question – they go off talking about this, that or the other, which is all fine so long as the money's coming in. Non-executives always like to talk about the culture in your business. Which is important. But not as important as making money.

Your back of the diary figures need to add up. Every day.

If they add up, fine. Let's talk culture.

If not, not so much.

Home From Home

One of the challenges with our first depots was to get them to feel like home. Not homely, but like home. Every depot had a television in it so that when a builder came in from out of the cold and the rain they'd have something to watch – the news or the sport, whatever. Something rather than nothing. We also

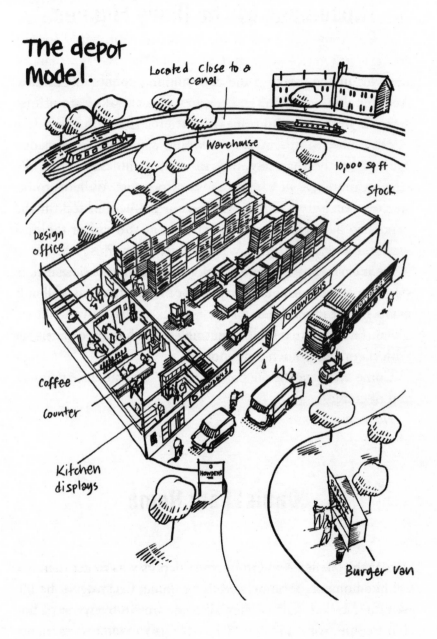

The depot Model.

Located close to a canal

Warehouse

10,000 sq ft

Stock

Design office

Coffee

Counter

Kitchen displays

Burger van

put a coffee machine in every depot, a proper coffee machine, and builders could help themselves.

A few home comforts in the depots: this probably sounds entirely straightforward and obvious. The average man or woman on the street could tell you that was a good idea. And yet at the beginning, even my suggestion of these little gestures were met with resistance. There are health and safety implications, Matthew, people would say. What if someone spills coffee on themselves? And what about the cost of the television licence, we can't possibly afford that. Well, of course we could afford that. And it wasn't as if I was asking for the depots to be decked out with armchairs and coffee tables. I wasn't asking for cosy – I was only asking for just enough to make it clear that we were a welcoming business. A gesture, a sign. For me it wasn't a nice thing to do. It was a must-have. It was a business decision.

You have to give people something to establish a relationship with them – not much, but enough.

Come on in out of the cold while we get your order. Quick cup of coffee?

Deal done.

Denis' Last Drink

All of these ideas – and I know they're pretty basic ideas, about common human decency, and things being worthwhile for all, Skipton Market Rules – they all come from somewhere. They don't come from nowhere. I haven't just made this stuff up. They come from my own experience and observations, they come from my reading and thinking, and they come from the many people I've been lucky enough to have known over the years. There will always be those people who you work with who influence your thinking about your business – that's to be expected – but there are also those people who have an impact on your thinking about your business who have nothing to do with your business. For me, Denis Watkins was one of those people.

Denis was the joint owner of the Angel Inn at Hetton, with John Topham. Denis and John were chefs – but they weren't just chefs. They were restaurateurs. They had a vision. And they saw it through.

Denis taught me a lot about quality, about service and about value – and about doing what you say you're going to do, consistently. What Denis and John did at the Angel Inn was remarkable. Before they arrived, the Angel Inn was an old wayside inn, an old-fashioned village boozer, rather down on its luck. They bought the place out of receivership and turned it into an award-winning brasserie, while somehow retaining its local clientele. No mean feat. This was long before gastropubs were a thing. Indeed, Denis is sometimes referred to as the Godfather of the Gastropub, an accolade he richly deserves.

Anyway, the Angel Inn was the place I always used to go and sit when I was working things through. It's the place where I found myself when I was between jobs. It's where I formulated the Howdens concept and the name and the logo. The Angel Inn is a special place – because Denis made it special.

As well as being a great chef and restaurateur, Denis also knew a thing or two about wine – he had a little house in Burgundy, in among the vineyards. He used to say that one of his great dreams was to have become a winemaker. He wanted everyone to be able to enjoy good wine. His principle was that he used to put £7 on a bottle of wine. So if you were drinking a cheap bottle of wine in the Angel, it cost you an extra £7 – and if you were drinking an expensive bottle of wine it still only cost you an extra £7. He was a man of his word, Denis. And he was a doer – I remember one year when I wanted to give the staff a hamper at Christmas, he said, I'll get that done for you, Matthew, and that was it, sorted. I didn't have to think about it again. Denis got it done.

A man of his word, serving good-quality food and wine – and a lovely man. Asked what he wanted his epitaph to be, Denis said, 'He created something which gave great pleasure to his fellow man'. Not a bad epitaph.

So when I discovered that Denis was ill I decided I wanted to do something for him, something that would give him great pleasure. At home I have a shed which is well stocked with some nice wines, and so I said to Denis, look, for a change why don't we have a little wine tasting here at the house. Let me treat you. That'd be lovely, Matthew, he said. And he agreed he'd come one Sunday after church – he was a serious Catholic, Denis. Anyway, he duly brought his wife Juliet and a few friends and between us we managed to work our way through about thirty bottles that Sunday. It was a great afternoon.

The following week I got a call from John Topham. It turned out that Denis went straight from our wine tasting to the hospital – and died shortly after.

I hadn't realised exactly how ill he was. I wondered if the wine tasting had been a good idea after all. I felt bad. But John Topham said that we had done Denis a great favour. It was how he would have wanted it.

It was a wonderful Sunday afternoon – a small thing to be able to do for a man who had created something which gave great pleasure to his fellow man.

Come Together

Restaurants like the Angel Inn have been an important part of my life in business. Restaurants tend to be where you meet people and talk to people, where you eat together and try and establish some sort of common feeling, some commonality. They are the natural home of conversation and discussion. They're where people come together.

Denis understood that. Denis understood that a restaurant is not just about the food: it's about the service, the ambience, the quality of care. Restaurants are not just about the food. A restaurant is about what happens there. Over the years there have been plenty of places that have been important to me and the business in this regard, places that have got it right. Nothing fancy, just right: Yann's restaurant in Crieff, where they have this chef from Chamonix, where everything's very cheesy and the tables are close together and the atmosphere is just perfect; Delvino's restaurant in Auchterarder, where they do a lovely pizza and a nice slice of cake; the King's Head in Kettlewell, where they only have about six tables and they write up what they've got on the blackboard and there's a tiny kitchen out the back and a fire going in the corner; the Alice Hawthorn Inn at Nun Monkton; the Cross Keys in East Marton; and Fino's in London.

Fino's has played such an important part in Howdens history that it probably deserves a chapter of its own. Fino's is proof that just one good meal in a good restaurant can make all the difference.

Our first few months of trading – October, November, December 1995 – were touch and go. In addition to our initial teething troubles, Magnet were sending people round to our managers, trying to recruit them back, offering them significant amounts of money to return. They were determined to put us out of business before we'd even really begun. Things were really quite challenging. Howdens was working less well than MFI had expected. I was under considerable pressure. I was constantly going round the depots, trying to get things going. I remember I was staying over somewhere in Dartford – it was maybe the Dartford Hilton, I can't remember – and I was checking in and I thought I could hear carols playing and for a moment I was disorientated, I couldn't work out why they were playing carols. I'd been working so hard I'd forgotten it was Christmas. And it was then that I realised that if I wasn't careful none of our staff would be coming back after Christmas. I was going to lose everyone.

This was early December 1995. I knew I needed to do something. I needed to boost morale. I rang a wine merchant and made sure that a case of good wine was sent out to each depot – and then I set about organising a Christmas party. I rang round everywhere, but everywhere was booked. I'd left it too late. So I rang my old friend Alan 'Ritzy' Davies. I need to organise a work Christmas party, I said. Right, said Ritzy, no problem. For next year, yes? For next week, I said. Leave it with me, said Ritzy. And half an hour later he rang back. I've spoken to Marco at Fino's on Mount Street, he said. He can fit you in, but he can only do lunch. That'll do, I said.

And so we gathered everyone together at Fino's on Mount Street – which is this amazing little family-run Italian place in Mayfair, reasonably priced, great food, outstanding service – and we had a wonderful meal and I remember when I came to pick up the bill my MFI credit card was rejected so I had to pay out of my own pocket. It was worth it.

Somehow we all got back home after the party and I checked in with Keith Sims that everyone was OK. Keith knew what was going on – he knew that I knew that everyone had offers to return to Magnet, and that we were facing difficulties, but Keith said everyone was fine. Everyone had enjoyed the party.

In the end, we didn't lose anyone at all over that Christmas. Everyone returned, and the business began to flourish. Fino's helped save us – and we have been going there ever since.

Is Mr Ingle There?

As business took off, I found myself increasingly having to stay overnight in hotels in London. Which sounds great. And which can be. Sometimes.

I would sometimes stay at the Connaught, in Mayfair, which is a very nice hotel. Very nice indeed. I was there once for business and my wife rang through – this was pre-mobile phones. The call was answered, my wife asked if Mr Ingle was there – and the husky-voiced receptionist replied, memorably, 'Not right now, honey, but I'm sure he'll be coming soon.' My wife promptly put the phone down. That's not really the way to answer the phone to a wife calling to check on her husband in a five-star hotel. You can perhaps imagine the subsequent conversation.

By way of apology, the Connaught offered us a complimentary weekend, with tickets to a show and dinner in the grill room – which was very decent of them. Except that when I was seated at the table and my wife was approaching, she was taken to one side by the maître d', who solemnly informed her that Mr Ingle was a very important guest here, that the hotel was very discreet, and that madam could be assured that nothing that went on here would go any further. Suffice it to say, we never stayed again.

There were plenty of other strange places I stayed in London over the years. There was the little boutique hotel which saw fit to provide guests with complimentary condoms, an Instamatic camera and a mask: you certainly don't get that in Harrogate. There was another place that had no locks on the doors and which seemed to cater entirely to German men carrying teddy bears on leads. And another where a couple were getting very intimate indeed over breakfast – which put me right off my bacon and eggs.

Rather fed up with all these metropolitan shenanigans, and after a particularly unpleasant stay in some strange place or other, I can remember getting into a taxi one night in September 2000 and asking the driver to simply take me round all the central London hotels until I could find a place where I might feel at home. I'm from Yorkshire, I explained. Right you are, sir.

We eventually ended up at Durrants – quiet, modest, unpretentious. I remember walking in for the first time: man on the door, fire in the grate, nice little bar and restaurant. Old-fashioned values. No funny business. It's been my base when I'm staying in London now for more than twenty years.

Take Down the Walls

Our business at Howdens is making kitchens, so it's no surprise that I've had a lot of conversations over the years with people about kitchens and kitchen design, and what works at home – and indeed in restaurants – and how to maximise space, and what's the best way to do this or that.

To be honest, as far as your domestic kitchen is concerned, most of the principles of kitchen design are pretty obvious. If you've got a dark kitchen, get some light cabinets. Nobody wants a dark kitchen. And don't forget the kitchen triangle: fridge, oven, sink. You don't want to be walking too far to your fridge. Make sure – if you can – that two people can work comfortably together in the kitchen at once. And think about where you're putting your cutlery drawer: the cutlery drawer can be the cause of all sorts of problems. If you want to get some serving spoons or a corkscrew and I'm standing in front of the cutlery drawer – well, that's going to be a problem.

But do you know what the most important thing in kitchen design is?

The most important thing in any kitchen design is – if you can – to take down as many walls as possible. Because a kitchen is not just there for cooking. A kitchen is not just a place to prepare food. It's much more than that. A kitchen is a multi-functional living space. It's a cliché to say it, but it's the centre of your home. You want to play a board game? Where are you going to play it? The dog has a tick on its leg? Where are you going to sort it out? You have some good news, some bad news? Where are you going to sit and talk it through? Someone's popped in to say hello. Someone needs help with their homework. Someone has to make a big decision. Where does all this tend to happen? In the kitchen.

The kitchen is a reception area, it's an entertaining area, a storage space, a call centre, a debate chamber, a reading room, a TV and cinema screening room, a business and computing centre, a lecture room, a surgery, an arena for all of life's arrivals and departures.

This means that kitchens are never really big enough. Just in terms of cooking utensils, people sometimes forget how many pots and pans need to be stored in a cupboard. In most kitchens, you open a cupboard, everything just comes tumbling out.

This wasn't always the case. When I was young, people often had just a little kitchenette or a scullery, with maybe a pantry, somewhere for the old twin tub. And that was it. But the way we live now, things have changed. These days, people want to be together. We can find our privacy via our screens, so the kitchen is increasingly the gathering place – it's where we come together. Because despite everything, humans still need each other, we crave each other's company, at home, in a restaurant. I remember when our children were young and we had a little cottage and their bedrooms were big enough but they always used to get dressed in the corridor: humans just like to know that other people are around.

So, here's my best advice when it comes to kitchen design, born of years in the business, and raising a family, and enjoying wonderful times in more restaurants than I could even begin to mention: take down the walls.

Hyper Local

Word started to spread about Howdens – but we needed it to spread faster and further. We decided to put our resources into direct marketing. And I mean very direct. I mean hyper local.

Before the depots had opened I'd gone to an old friend, an advertising man called Peter Boggs, and he'd put together a direct marketing campaign for us. Peter is a brilliant ad man. A great marketeer. And I thought the direct marketing campaign we put together was absolutely great.

Unfortunately, it turned out to be a complete and utter waste of time. It was a total failure. It just didn't work. We did our best. But it didn't work.

Basically, our idea was that we'd do a local mail shot round the new Howden depots, announcing the opening of the business, inviting people to come in and buy something, and they'd get a free gift. The first person to buy this or that gets a microwave or a radio, etc. We sent the mail shots centrally from MFI. And in our first week, the week beginning 4 October 1995, precisely no one came in to claim their free gift. No one. Not a soul. I couldn't understand it. I checked with the MFI marketing department. Are you sure it's gone out? Oh yes, yes, it's gone out.

It had gone out – but it hadn't worked.

Which is when I decided that at Howdens we would have no central marketing at all, direct or not.

Direct marketing is of course excellent in principle – why bother with third party publications and the mass media when you can communicate directly with your target audiences? Cut out the middle man and go direct – via mail shots, or these days social media, email, phone/SMS campaigns, whatever. It's a good idea.

The problem is, even with direct marketing, if it's a centralised system you are ceding your responsibility for telling people about your product or service to someone else. It may be more targeted than some big national advertising campaign in the print and broadcast media, but it's still someone else doing the targeting for you.

I decided that the local depot managers needed to take full responsibility for finding their customers. I told them to go through their local Yellow Pages, to design their own mail shot, to put it in an envelope, to handwrite the address and put a stamp on it. No franking machines. No head office involvement at all – because if the local manager owns it, the chances are, it's going to work. Your customer will know it comes from an actual person in an actual depot, rather than from some faceless corporate machine. Oh, and when you've sent out your personal local mail shot, you need to follow it up personally with a personal phone call – direct from the local depot to the local builder.

In terms of our marketing, the decision to go from centralised direct marketing to hyper local changed everything.

Ogilvy Direct

Really the principle of hyper local direct marketing was just me applying the principles I'd learnt from the greatest advertising man of the twentieth century, David Ogilvy.

I first went looking for David in 1986, when I was still at Magnet. I was dissatisfied with J. Walter Thompson, who were our advertising agency at the time. We needed a change. And I happened to see a programme on TV about advertising and Ogilvy was on and he was like a breath of fresh air. After years of listening to all sorts of nonsense from ad people I thought this bloke Ogilvy sounded like he knew what he was talking about. He was the only advertising man I'd ever heard who actually made any sense.

Advertising, according to Ogilvy, is just about the facts. It's not about being creative or clever. It's about presenting the facts as clearly as possible. You treat your customers with respect. You explain your product to them clearly. Being sophisticated and smart is totally irrelevant – because nobody cares. Sophistication does not equal intelligence. Advertising is not about manipulation, it's about articulation. Your job is to tell the truth. You can guarantee that nothing will fail quicker than a well-advertised bad product – so just get the product right, and then tell the truth about the product. This was music to my ears.

So I went to J. Walter Thompson and asked if they could put me in touch with this Mr Ogilvy, whoever he was, and they said no, he's retired to France and he's not involved in advertising any more and he'll never talk to you. Oh right, I said, fine. And I just found his address and wrote to him and about a week later he replied, inviting me to visit him at home in France, and if I brought with me some of our catalogues and ads and what have you we could go through it together. Which is what I did. I went to Ogilvy direct.

A few weeks later I turned up in France, he picked me up, took me to his extraordinary home, the Château de Touffou, which is really more like a castle, and I spent an evening being given a masterclass in advertising by David Ogilvy. Tell the truth, said David. Tell the story. Forget about branding. Forget about being clever and original. Focus on your core ideas and your core offering – and articulate it. Forget about national advertising. It's a waste of time and money. You need to go direct.

Important lessons which have served us well at Howdens, thanks to David.

Stories, Myths and Legends

Another important idea at Howdens that was influenced by David Ogilvy's insights about the power of clear articulation is that everybody throughout our business should be able to understand the story of the business and be able to tell the story of the business.

Explaining your story is not about brand values, it's not about fancy language and big ideas. It's about explaining what you do, and why. So, for Howdens, if I had to sum up our story, I'd say that we are a company who make kitchens in our factories which we sell to tradesmen through our depots, where we treat our staff well and reward them properly. That's about it. That's what we do – in a language that people can understand.

Simple messaging. That's why I've always found Nelson so interesting. I can remember studying Nelson at school and being particularly struck by the stories of how he communicated his ideas: 'England expects that every man will do his duty', the signal sent from his flagship HMS *Victory* on

21 October 1805 at the Battle of Trafalgar; or his famous final message, 'Engage the enemy more closely'. These are messages that everyone can understand. They're like signposts – big and clear. If you go this way, you're not going to go badly wrong. We don't need to sketch in all the details – we don't have time to sketch in all the details. You can work out the details for yourself. But in the grand scheme of things, if you get the general gist of the message, you're going to be heading in the right direction.

These principles apply to all sorts of stories. Carl Jung has this idea about the collective unconscious – I read Jung years ago and I was fascinated by his ideas. If all the fairy tales in the world disappeared overnight, in Jung's reckoning, and we all got back together again the next day, the basic stories would soon re-emerge. The parable of the burying of the talents, the goose that laid the golden egg, Icarus, the stories of dying and resurrected gods. The great myths and legends represent a profound understanding of what life is truly like. Stories and parables address the great mysteries of life, and they give us access to fundamental truths.

I remember the deputy head at my prep school, a man named Arthur Hibbert – he flew a Hurricane at the Battle of Britain. Mr Hibbert taught us history and sport and he always used to say, boys, you need to learn how to tell stories. People will always remember stories, they won't always remember the facts.

Successful businesses tend to be guided by certain principles and ideas – and for me one of the best ways of explaining my ideas and principles to people has been through telling stories. I have always enjoyed reading books of fables and myths, and I have used them often to illustrate various ideas at Howdens over the years. There are far too many to list, but here are just three of my favourites, stories that I've told people a thousand times. You'll get the gist.

First, the fable of the donkey and his load of salt – one of Aesop's fables. There's a donkey labouring in a hot climate – he's struggling with a load on his back, his master is driving him hard. And one day he has to cross a river. He enters the river and begins to make his way across, but Donkey stumbles and falls. He almost drowns, but he manages to get up onto his feet and finds that his load is light. He carries on with his journey, and it's easy. It's extraordinary – he thinks he's gone to heaven. He eventually returns to his stable and then the following day he comes out and has another load put on his back. This time, he stumbles and falls deliberately in the river, expecting his load again to lighten and so his journey to be easy. But this time the load grows heavy – and he drowns. On the first day, Donkey was carrying salt – and the water washed away the heavy load. On the second day he was carrying sponges – and the water added to his burden. Just because it worked today, doesn't mean it's going to work tomorrow. Beware complacency and false assumptions.

Second, the story of the monkey and the fishermen – another of Aesop's fables. Monkey is watching some fishermen out on their boat – he is fascinated by the fishermen throwing out their nets and hauling them back in, full of fish. And Monkey thinks, I can do that. And when the fishermen go home that night, he paddles out to their boat, gets hold of the net, throws it out, gets tangled up – and drowns. It might look easy but unless you know what you're doing you can get into serious trouble.

And finally, the parable of the burying of the talents, one of those wonderful strange stories in the Gospels. A master is going on a long journey and so he entrusts his property to his servants – the property is divided into parts, which is worth so much money, or talents. Upon returning home after a long absence, the master asks his servants for an account of the talents he has entrusted to them. The first and the second servants have put their talents to work and have doubled their value. These servants are duly rewarded. But the third servant has simply buried his talent – and he gets cast into outer darkness, where there is weeping and wailing and gnashing of teeth. A lack of courage, of learning, of adventurousness – in the end it will be punished.

Good stories. True stories.

Avoid All Offices and PAs

There were all sorts of things at Howdens that I decided to do differently: the company structure, the bonus scheme, the direct local marketing, the way we told our stories. I also decided I wouldn't have an office – because I knew that if I had an office I'd end up having a PA.

Not that there is anything wrong with having a PA. I have the greatest respect for PAs. My wife is a PA. And I have had some excellent PAs – Loretta, Vicki, Patricia. Absolutely extraordinary people. Brilliant people. Essential to the running of a business.

But the trouble is, at the end of the day, a PA has one thing to do – which is to find you things to do. And in business the only person who should be deciding what to do is you, not somebody else. Also, a PA is a colleague – which means they need looking after, when you should really be concentrating on the business. These are lessons I learnt from that old crook and worktop innovator George Reynolds. PAs are all well and good, George used to say, but what makes them all well and good is exactly what makes them a very big problem: they want to look after you. The first thing they do is to start organising things for you, and then of course they need to do some typing, so you need a stationery cupboard, and then you need someone to look after the stationery cupboard and before you know it you've got a whole Stationery Cupboard Department and a Stationery Cupboard Purchasing Department and then you have to get an HR Department to deal with the problems in the Stationery Cupboard Purchasing Department, and a PR Department to be able to deal with the press about the HR Department's treatment of the Stationery Cupboard Purchasing Department and the whole thing just gets out of control very quickly.

So, PAs are wonderful. And offices are lovely.

But I decided I wouldn't have an office or a PA.

However, MFI insisted on giving me a PA. They couldn't understand how anyone could survive without one. They gave me a PA.

That arrangement lasted approximately ten days. I made it clear that it wasn't going to work. I knew what I needed to do, and I knew how I needed to do it.

In all the years I was running Howdens all I used was a Nokia C2-01. A basic mobile phone. Not a smartphone. And no computer. I had no iPhone, no laptop, no gadgets or tools, no nothing. Just me, the Nokia C2-01 – and the Z graph. The Z graph was the only other tool I needed.

Z Graphs

Now: the Z graph. This really is the nitty gritty.

The Z graph is probably the most powerful tool in any CEO's toolbox – honestly. If I had to pick one tool – one thing, one insight – that helped me in my career at Howdens, it'd be the Z graph. The Z graph is like black magic and alchemy combined. It gives you total visibility of your daily numbers. And in business, visibility is good. You don't want smoke and mirrors. You don't want fog. You don't want darkness. You don't want shade. You want it all out in the open. In business, you want things to be transparent. You want things to be clear. You want to know where you are, where you've been, and where you're going.

Like most things in business, this is of course completely obvious and utterly simple – and yet most people are neither brave nor honest enough to face the truth that a tool like the Z graph reveals. The Z graph won't give you the answers, but it does give you the truth – and the truth will lead you to the answers.

If you apply Skipton Market Rules and you attend to your daily Z graph, your business is not going to go far wrong.

And yet in every business I have ever worked in – every single one – no one seems to want to do the basic daily numbers. Do you not want to know what your daily figures are? No? Really? Because your daily figures become your monthly totals, which become your quarterlies, and then your annual sales and turnover and profit and projections. The daily figures are essential. They're foundational. They are the business.

The problem seems to be that most people, when they look at numbers, immediately want to interpret them. They want to discuss them. When people look at the numbers in business they always tend to say, it just depends on how you look at them. No, no, no. It doesn't depend how you look at them. Numbers are numbers, and facts are facts. So, let's say in January you did £200 worth of business. In February you did £205. In March, £195. And in April, £190. Given those four numbers, what do you think the number is going to be for May? Is it going to be £250? No? Is it going to be £150? Unlikely. It's probably going to be between about £190 and £210, isn't it? So, now we know where we are and what we've got to do. It's basic maths. Even I can do it.

The Z graph, or the Z chart, so-called because the pattern on such a chart forms a rough letter Z, is a method of formalising these sorts of simple calculations, allowing you to view your numbers up close, in the short term, and in the mid-term, and in the long term. It is an incredibly powerful tool.

There are three lines represented in the Z graph. There's the current line, which is the short-term variation for each period – say, a day, or a month. Then there's your moving total, which is mid-term figure, and which allows you to see any seasonal variations. And there's the all-important cumulative line, which combines these figures and adds them to your annual figures and so allows you to see your long-term progress.

The bottom line alone of the Z graph is going to make you pay attention to what needs to happen tomorrow or next month. And then if you look at the cumulative mid-line, well, you can put your ruler on that, and you can see how your year is progressing, if things are going to be OK, so you can plan for that. And then when you look at the top line, the annualised figures, you're able to see not just the mid-term

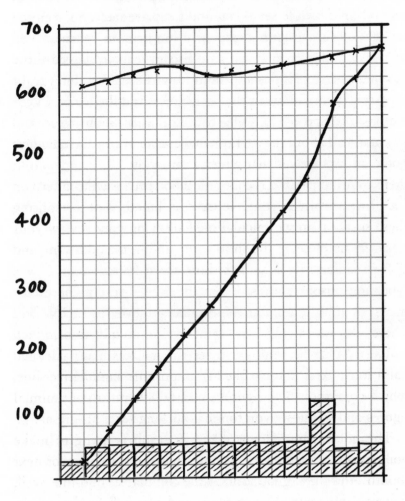

Z GRAPH 2006

progress, but where you are heading as a business over time, up and down.

You can see that the Z graph is a hugely powerful tool. It's a multi-tool: in one small chart you're measuring three things. Which means as soon as you get an up-tick or a down-tick, you've got a whole set of numbers represented and you can see if it's just a monthly blip or a longer-term issue, and so then – and only then – you can discuss reality. These are the numbers. Here's all the information we need. You don't want excessive data. You want the basic facts. And then armed with the basic facts you ask, well, what do we do about it?

I first read about the Z graph in some dusty old management book on my shelves many many years ago, so I understood them in principle, but the person who really taught me about the power of the Z graph in making big decisions was John Foulkes, the man who was brought into Magnet when it was all going wrong.

I remember we'd had a very good month and I was reporting on our figures. I thought things were going pretty well, but John looked at the numbers and he just exploded. There was me saying everything was fine and he said, no, actually, Matthew, you are in serious trouble. Your sales are going backwards. Backwards? I didn't understand. How could they be going backwards? We did really well this month, I said. Look at the moving annual total, he said. Look at the Z graph. And there it was, plain to see. You are simply not making enough money. Over time, your sales are going down. What are you going to do about it?

The Z graph is like the mirror on the wall. If you ask it, it will tell you the truth. And in business, you have to be prepared to face the truth.

Flip Charts

So I was never a great one for all the fancy business bells and whistles – the PAs, the fancy offices, the glossy business plans and brochures, the big talk, the razzamatazz. My idea of doing a presentation was sketching a few ideas on a flip chart, and then getting on with things. I am a man who has never knowingly designed a PowerPoint.

Anyway, Derek Hunt's successor as Chief Executive at MFI was a man named John Hancock, and John came to the conclusion that Howdens needed to be presented properly to the City. We needed to get the message out there. We needed to tell our story. So I said, fine. That's no problem, John. I'll go round and do a presentation using a flip chart. But John did not think that was a good idea: he thought we needed something a bit more professional-looking, a bit more slick.

So I was introduced to a communications expert, a woman named Roxy Fry. Roxy is quite something. She lives in France, works in London and New York, she was somehow connected with breakfast TV, and she used to work with some heavy metal band. She's an eccentric, Roxy, a character. She teaches people like me how to do pitches and presentations, events, conferences, reports – everything. She's a master storyteller. And she was tasked with teaching me the art of the slick presentation. So I sat down with Roxy and she asked me how I liked to do things and I showed her my flip chart – and she advised that I should keep using the flip chart. Matthew, she said, you're going to need to do it your way. We developed it a bit, obviously – she taught me a few tricks of the flip chart trade. She helped me organise my diagrams, and how to keep things neat and tidy. But at the end of the day, it was a flip chart. And the flip chart triumphed.

When eventually there was a big crisis with MFI, in 2005, I had to go round doing presentations to shareholders. I had to try and calm things down. But rather than attempting some big glossy presentation we stuck to the flip charts and I went round to people individually and talked them through the options – and I found that by talking normally and calmly, jotting down a few simple notes on the old flip charts, all these furiously angry people would suddenly sit and listen. It was the opposite of razzamatazz and slick: it was honest and it was simple. And it bought us valuable time. We managed to sort things out.

It was a tremendous lesson. Don't overdo it. Do what comes naturally. And if you're a flip chart kind of a person, use a flip chart.

The Little White Books

Flip charts are fine, but as Howdens grew I had to find ways of communicating with more and more people about our core principles and ideas – our stories. I couldn't be hauling a flip chart around to every depot and factory. Which is when I had the idea of the Little White Book.

You'll doubtless be familiar with Chairman Mao's famous *Little Red Book* – or, to give its full title, *Quotations from Chairman Mao Zedong*, originally produced in 1964 by the People's Liberation Army and distributed to every Chinese citizen. 'Every Communist must grasp the truth: Political power grows out of the barrel of a gun.' 'All reactionaries are paper tigers. In appearance, the reactionaries are terrifying, but in reality they are not so powerful.' Etc, etc.

I don't agree with the ideas in Mao's *Little Red Book*. To say the least. But I liked the idea of some kind of little guide to our business. So we produced a couple of editions of what I called our Little White Book – which was literally just a little white book, distributed to all staff. The books are basically reproductions of my hand drawn flip chart presentations – my vision of the business, written by me, by hand, for everyone to be able to see and refer to if and when necessary, a kind of Howdens handbook.

Original? No.

Useful? Yes.

By Hand

My writing was never really very good – and I mean my actual handwriting, never mind the grammar and punctuation. It was an absolute mess. Which was never really a problem in the old days when I was at Magnet and you'd have typists and secretaries to take care of all that. But when things really started getting going with Howdens there was literally no time for typing things up and sending out memos – and I didn't have a PA. So we'd have a meeting, I'd take the minutes, write them up, and that was it. It was more like jot down a few thoughts, photocopy them and hand them round.

And it was at that point – trying to decipher my own scrawl – that I realised that I needed to smarten up my writing. So

I taught myself how to write from a little booklet, *How to Write Like This: An Introduction to the Art of Calligraphy*, published by the Derwent Cumberland Pencil Company. It remains to this day one of the most purely useful business books I have ever read.

Four Points

If the Derwent Cumberland Pencil Company and Roxy Fry taught me everything I needed to know about the art of communicating on paper, Susan Gilchrist taught me everything I know about how to perform in front of a crowd.

If you're running a public limited company – a company whose ownership is organised by shares of stock – you have to learn how to perform at a whole series of presentations to shareholders and analysts and journalists.

Shareholder presentations are a kind of ritual. They're an important part of the business cycle. What happens is that you give a quick outline of the business, you cover the main points and then you hand over to your Chief Financial Officer, who spends about fifteen minutes going through the figures, and then you summarise what's been said, expand a little bit, and then you take questions. You have to get it *exactly* right. There is no room for error. With a public company, you cannot express an opinion about what's likely to be happening in the future, in case it influences the market. But the people in the room are desperate for a sign or a signal – they're reading your body language, they're picking up on every little hint and tell, because they are there to buy or sell. They want to know which way the wind is blowing. Whatever you say, they're going to read it and interpret it and pick it over and come to their own conclusions. You need a poker face. You need to tell the story straight, and tell it right, and yet not give too much away.

So, for example, let's say you're in retail and you're doing a presentation and you say that your larger stores have done really well – people will instantly work out that this means that your smaller stores may have done less well, which means that you might be closing them, which will affect your turnover, which will have consequences for the share price and within seconds – seconds – people will have jumped to all sorts of conclusions. They'll have made up their minds.

It's a very tricky business. I've seen Chief Executives slip up – you make some off-hand remark about your business and your share price goes rocketing up, and then you have to issue a statement and the share price collapses. It can all get very messy very quickly. You have to be extremely careful.

At Howdens, Susan Gilchrist – of the Brunswick Group, the big advisory firm – was the person who helped to keep me on message when I was talking to shareholders and analysts and journalists. Matthew, all you need to remember, Susan would say, is that every question, no matter how difficult, is really just an opportunity to tell your story. And when you're telling that story, just remember, you only have four points. You learn them, and then you just go round those four points, again and again and again. Ad infinitum. You don't go off message, you don't go off script, you don't improvise, elaborate, you don't make things up on the spot. Before a big presentation, Susan would help to drill me on the points so that when it came to speaking to the shareholders and journalists I was entirely consistent in what I said.

Like Roxy, Susan stuck with me at Howdens until the end. In business, you develop relationships of trust with some people, people who you can rely on in a crisis. Sometimes in business things happen very quickly and you have to react. I remember more than once on a Sunday evening, meeting at Susan's office and going through all the details of something before the markets opened on the Monday morning. Susan saved us from a lot of difficulties and embarrassments.

Business isn't really about being clever, or daring. It's often about being cautious and clear. It's about simple messages, endlessly repeated. You have to be ready, you have to be clear. And it helps if you have someone like Susan to remind you to stick to your four points.

Mateus Rosé

The challenge of learning how to do fancy presentations to the City is one thing. The day-to-day challenges of running a business are another thing entirely. For me, in the early days at Howdens, that meant building a culture that we could be proud of. And unlikely as it sounds, Mateus Rosé had an important part to play in the development of that culture.

As the business grew, I spent a lot of time out on the road, visiting the depots, week in, week out, driving the length and breadth of the country. It was very important to me that when I visited I was able to sit down with people as equals, to be able to talk entirely freely, in a frank and honest way about the business: no bullshit, no kow-towing, proper honest conversations. So early on I devised a modest tradition that I believe remains as effective and useful today as it ever was in establishing and maintaining our business culture: the curry night.

Each region was encouraged to have a monthly curry night, with all the depot managers required to be present. A local curry house would be chosen, and the meal would start early and be scheduled to last only a couple of hours, so that people could get home to be with their families. We'd sit down, there'd be a quick round-up of the state of play – progress on targets, any problems or issues arising – and then the rest of the night was given over to a bit of chat while enjoying a curry and a bottle or two of Mateus Rosé.

You cannot beat a nice bottle of Mateus Rosé – pale pink, medium-sweet, slightly fizzy. The uniquely shaped bottle is modelled on an old army flask. A 1970s classic – a favourite of the Queen's, I believe – this is not a fancy wine. It is not a connoisseur's wine. It is a wine that just about everyone can enjoy. Cold and with a curry, it's absolutely perfect.

I always used to time my visits to coincide with the curry nights in different regions – I'd do two or three curry nights a week. It was a good way of catching up with people. What could be better? A nice curry and a few glasses of a nice unpretentious wine that when cold goes very well with Indian food. It gave me the chance to stay abreast of what was happening in the business, and it gave people the opportunity to raise any issues directly with me.

Also, the great thing about Indian food is that you share it among you – it's not a case of I'm having steak and she's having vegetarian lasagne, and never the twain shall meet. And while we're at it, let's not chug down the beers or the double vodkas. This is not a drinking competition: this is a convivial evening among colleagues. The curry nights

Curry nights

Curry nights gave a forum to informally discuss issues of the day, and were held up and down the country in every region.

Once a year an award was presented to the region that was judged to have provided the best curry experience.

provided a way of modelling the kind of behaviour that I like to think characterised the spirit of Howdens: civilised, polite, not pretentious or showy. I loved every minute of it – fuelled by Mateus Rosé.

The Car Coat

When I was at school back in the early 1960s I remember there was a master who turned up and caused a bit of a commotion.

Everything back then was still a bit run-down, it was still post-war, pre-Beatles. Things were a bit dull. And then Mr Wilkinson arrived. The thing about Mr Wilkinson was, you could actually smell him – because he wore cologne. Cologne! None of us had ever encountered a man who wore cologne. And he had properly barbered hair. And he wore these smart grey flannels, and proper sports jackets – not just some flap of tweed with leather patches, like the other teachers. He was a terribly smartly dressed man, Mr Wilkinson. Suede shoes with crepe soles. He was utterly distinctive. He had a look.

He was our Latin master. But his great claim to fame – apart from the way he looked – was that he drove a Bentley. Teachers back then did not generally drive Bentleys. They certainly don't drive Bentleys now. But then Mr Wilkinson was a gambling man – which was said to be the source of his Bentley-buying riches. He would watch the racing on the television on a Saturday afternoon with us. But he eventually sold the Bentley and turned up at school one day driving a Mini Clubman, with a telephone and a gramophone in it – which caused yet another sensation. None of us had ever seen a Mini Clubman, never mind one that was fitted out with all mod cons. He brought colour to a grey world, Mr Wilkinson.

There were all these things about him. The car he drove. The way he dressed. Even the way he marked our papers. He had an extraordinary way of grading people. He had about six Parker pens in his pockets, all different colours, all with the corresponding ink, and he would draw these symbols on your homework. He had this complex colour-coded grading system. Eventually you could work out what mark you'd received, but you had to work at it – so even the homework became a bit of an adventure. And if you did well, he didn't just give you a double tick or a gold star – he had a big box of sweets.

I never learnt much Latin from Mr Wilkinson but I did learn some other important lessons from him. He had a big impact on my thinking – a disproportionate impact. I don't really know why – perhaps it was because he was the first person I'd ever met who had really thought about self-projection and presentation, and who had made some decisions on the basis of his thinking. He was someone who understood the power of symbols. He was someone who understood that sometimes it's important to stand out, to make a bit of an impression, to give people something to talk about, and to offer rewards that are a little bit out of the ordinary. He understood that actions are louder than words.

In the early days at Howdens I always used to wear a tie with an old sweater, but I also needed a jacket. I needed something that I could wear around the depots on a daily basis. People in trade don't want to see a bloke coming in wearing a fancy suit – it sends the wrong message. And it's just not very practical. So I started wearing a sort of bomber jacket – but I quickly progressed to a light suede car coat. It was from Timberland. It wasn't cheap. It was quite something. I can still remember the day I bought it. If it's suede, I asked, is it waterproof? Of course it's waterproof, said the woman in the shop. And she promptly lay the coat down on the floor and threw a glass of water on it – and it ran off it like water off a duck's back. No need to wrap it up, I said. I'll take it. I loved that coat. It wasn't too heavy. It wasn't too hot. It was the perfect coat. I wore it all the time. It gave people something to talk about – Matthew's funny coat. For years I wore that coat. And I always drove the same car – a big old heavy Mercedes-Benz. Matthew's funny coat, and his big old car. It gave people certainty. They knew what to expect. I owe that to Mr Wilkinson.

Presence

For me, the first few years at Howdens were all about presence. If you're running a business you have to be present. You have to be around. You have to be there. And here, there – everywhere. Obviously we had board meetings once a week – I was always there. You had to be physically present to be able to pick up on the mood and every little nuance, the body language, everything.

It was the same with the depots. I had to be present at the depots. To me, there was just no choice. There was no alternative. You had to establish your networks and your connections. You had to know your people and what they were thinking and feeling. You had to be there to listen – and in order to establish your authority. You had to get to know people – and allow yourself to be known. You had to stand shoulder to shoulder with them, and demonstrate that you were able to act when action was required. So if you were at a depot and a manager had a problem, you could ring from the depot and explain what the problem was and get it sorted. You can lead from the front all you like – but you also have to be present.

Being present also greatly reduces the risk of misinterpretation. You know what it's like working in an office, or working anywhere – people say they've heard this or that. Workplaces are rumour mills. All sorts of crazy stuff gets said in the workplace – the gossip runs wild, and before you know it you've got a serious problem. But if you're actually there, if you're actually present, you can put a stop to all that. People have heard this or that. She's said this. He's said that. Well, no, you can say. Actually, that's not true. The truth is this.

I remember once we were introducing a new IT system into Howdens. There was this roll-out that was supposed to be completed in three months. But the team at the Watford depot were having problems with it – and they were making a terrible fuss. This didn't work, that didn't work. So I went to Watford and talked to them, listened to them, and then from there I called our IT department and told them to stop the roll-out until they'd fixed the problem.

If you're present, if you know the people, you can fix the problem.

And if you're not, and you don't, then you can't. And you won't.

Period 11

If you can't be there, you need people you can trust to be there. For me, one of those people was Andy Witts.

Andy is a mild-mannered genius. He'd been a depot manager at Magnet, and then he came over to Howdens and opened up our depots in Cardiff and Hereford – but he had bigger ambitions. I remember I was sitting in a curry house with him once and I asked him what he'd really like to do in the business and he said if he could he'd like to run the whole country. If someone like Andy says they want to do something like that then you're already halfway to succeeding – because someone like Andy only says what he means, and he does what he says. He progressed incredibly quickly through the business – from two depots to area manager, and then joint Managing Director with Chris Youell. He's now Chief Operating Officer of the trade division.

Andy's a fixer. He'll always find a way. The story goes that he was doing Father Christmas one year for some charity and a grandmother brought along her grandson to see Father Christmas and she tells him that he's been a very bad boy and doesn't deserve a present. Quick as a flash, Andy gets on the phone and pretends to ask some advice from his elves and they decide between them that the boy can have a present. Problem? Andy: solution.

At Howdens it was Andy who invented what we call our period 11 sale, the autumn sale, which has been a lifesaver for the business. People in our trade always used to run winter sales, but if you think about it, that doesn't make much sense. A winter sale might work if you're Harrods, but not so much if you're Howdens. For us, an autumn sale makes much more sense. In our business, in October no one is on holiday, it's still warm and dry outside, you can work from six till six – so *that*'s when we really need to sell to builders. That's when we need to offer everything we can to our customers. Andy Witts trialled what we call the period 11 concept in 1997 – and we've never looked back. Basically we say, look, Mr Builder, we've got these kitchens, we'll do you discount, do you want them now, yes or no? It's the right time of year for them – they can get their jobs planned for after Christmas, before they take a break. Their customers know they're going to be getting a kitchen. And we can steal a march on our competitors. Everyone's a winner.

So – have faith and trust in your colleagues, find those people with ambition and ideas, give them the opportunities and the confidence, and you won't go wrong. You'll find your Andy Witts.

Planes, Trains and Automobiles

In the early days at Howdens – in fact, for all of my days at Howdens – it was a pretty long working week. I'd usually get up around 4 a.m. on a Monday morning and I'd be off going round depots all week – drive home around Friday lunchtime, enjoy the weekend, and then start all over again. It was good fun. I enjoyed the travel. I got to see the whole of England. And Scotland. And Wales. And bits of Northern Ireland. It was pretty gruelling, but it was essential – it wasn't a luxury.

Anyway, at a certain point it just wasn't practical for me to be driving round the country any more. There were too many depots and not enough time, so John Hancock, the MFI Chief Executive, who replaced Derek Hunt, suggested that we sort ourselves out with a little plane. Which we did – this was via Ritzy Davies again. Ritzy found us a chap called Tony Beynon – a man with a few planes and plenty of experience. He was an old hand, Tony. I remember him telling me once that he was flying a plane across the Atlantic that ran out of fuel and it was only as he was plummeting down to the sea that he realised his elbow had caught the tap and all he had to do was turn the fuel back on again. He had nerves of steel, Tony – and a great sense of humour.

With Tony we ended up with a 1973 Beechcraft Baron. You might want to look it up, the old Beech Baron. (If you look it up on Wikipedia, the entry reads, 'There have been numerous accidents and incidents involving the Beechcraft Baron. Listed below are a select few of the most notable ones.' It is not exactly encouraging.) It's a twin engine low-wing monoplane, the Beech Baron. Executive jet it is not; it's pretty basic. It has just enough room for the pilot, with four tiny little seats in the back, and a cargo door. It's a bit like flying in a Spitfire or a Hurricane.

I absolutely loved it. Some colleagues simply refused to get in it – when they saw it they just refused. Understandably. But we had some great adventures. I remember we were in France once, flying back from Lille to Leeds Bradford, and it was the middle of winter, pitch black, absolute darkness, and it started raining. And I could hear Tony talking to the control tower, '273 Tango Bravo to tower, requesting permission to start engines.' Then it started snowing. '273 Tango Bravo to tower, requesting permission to start engines.' And then there was a blizzard. '273 Tango Bravo to tower, requesting permission to start engines.' 'Permission granted.' And off we went – into an absolute white-out. I've never seen anything like it before or since. It was the most terrifying journey of my life.

When we landed at Leeds Bradford and I got a taxi home the driver could not believe we'd arrived – we were the only plane in. All the runways were closed. The whole place was shut down. You must be more important than the police, he said. Or more foolish. It wasn't the sort of plane that a proper Chief Executive should be flying in, the Beechcraft Baron – but it did the job.

For touring the depots I also had a Jaguar saloon and an old Mercedes G-Wagon — they were absolutely perfect. Monday morning, carphone all plumbed in, overnight bag, and off you went.

It wasn't easy on family life, but I never really minded the actual travelling. It was all for a purpose. I even used to enjoy travelling in and out of King's Cross on the train, down from Doncaster into London. King's Cross was always a bit grimy, but there was something about it: home of the old Great Northern Railway, entryway to the north. At King's Cross you were either going home or you were arriving. And there were always other people going somewhere too – everyone travelling together, that sense of shared purpose. For me, that's what it was all about.

The A1

I spent so much of my working life on the road – it's amazing, thinking back on it. Hours, days, months spent travelling.

The A1 was always my favourite – one of the truly great roads. There's always a sense of excitement when you join the A1, that sense of going somewhere, of embarking upon a journey, that sense of becoming a part of the vast stream of history, stretching back all the way to the Romans. The Old North Road. The Great North Road. The M1 is really just there for convenience's sake, but the A1 is a proper old trade route, with all these staging posts along the way, with the old inns and taverns providing essential stabling for coach horses and replacement mounts: the Angel Inn at Wetherby; the Angel and Royal at Grantham; the George of Stamford; the Golden Lion at Ferrybridge; Ye Olde Bell at Barnby Moor; and of course the Ram Jam Inn in Rutland, haunt of Dick Turpin – and Harry Wright's Aylesbury duck.

The Meaning of Gleneagles

If you go all the way up the A1 to Edinburgh and then you drive another hour or so north you'll come to a little town called Auchterarder, the Lang Toun, or the Long Town, home to the famous Gleneagles Hotel.

Our first trip together as a team to Gleneagles was a transformative moment in the history of Howdens.

I remember when we first opened in 1995 I said we'd go to Gleneagles that year if we did well enough – but we didn't do well enough. We didn't do very well at all. So we didn't go.

But in 1996, when the depots were turning over stock as fast as they could get it in, we did. It was the right time to reward our early pioneers. And I'm proud to say that our Gleneagles event has taken place in the first week of December ever since. It's not exactly a Christmas party, nor is it exactly a conference: it's a reward for a job well done.

When we go to Gleneagles people spend the first two days fishing, or clay pigeon shooting, or having a massage, or whatever it is that takes their fancy. Then we have a nice dinner in the evening, silver service, the full works – and whichever area in the business has done the best numbers, they get to stay an extra night.

Our trip to Gleneagles is a signal to our staff that what we're doing is working, and an acknowledgement that any success is down to them – you don't take your depot managers to Gleneagles if your business isn't doing well. And again, it's a way of demonstrating the kind of ethos that I've always tried to instil: if you work hard then you can play hard, in the right spirit, at the right time, and together. For me, the annual trip to Gleneagles is an acknowledgement that everyone in a business wants to feel a part of something special – really special. This is Gleneagles, after all. It's not just your local pub, or some corporate hotel off the M6.

Also, going to Gleneagles enables our staff to see how things are done at their very best. At Gleneagles you get the very best service, the way it should be done: not too overbearing, but with an unbelievable level of attention to detail; a lovely relaxed atmosphere that is also rather formal and restrained; services and amenities of the highest order, but nothing silly or showy. It's just – well, it's perfect. I want our staff to learn from that example, and also to learn to feel comfortable in that environment. To be able to cope in a new and different environment – an environment which might at first appear strange and intimidating – is an important life skill. At Gleneagles our depot managers and teams find themselves mixing with captains of industry, with the very wealthy and the well-to-do. Our people come from all walks of life, from all sorts of backgrounds, and they go to work every day dealing with the Great British Public in all its great variety. And unlikely as it sounds, Gleneagles – in all its luxury, with its five-star accommodation, its golf course, its incredible facilities – has helped to teach our people how to behave not only among themselves on a luxury weekend away but also with the public in our humble Howdens depots all across the country, day in and day out, all throughout the year.

In the early days I remember I said, one year this business is going to be big enough to take over the whole hotel. And people said we'd never be big enough. Now of course the hotel isn't big enough for us. In the early days at Gleneagles, when we were a small team, we'd get up to all sorts of high jinks among ourselves: we'd play rugby in the private dining room and yes, people sometimes had a bit too much to drink. But do you know what? The great thing about Gleneagles is that nothing was ever too much trouble, and they have always welcomed us. I think our people have learnt more about how to run a business from a couple of days a year at Gleneagles than any number of training courses and away days.

So, don't waste your money on consultants and reports.

Take your team to Gleneagles.

Solutions, Not Problems

One of my most vivid memories of all my years at Howdens is arriving at Gleneagles railway station in the snow. I think it illustrates the value of those outings.

It was December 2010, our annual get-together. Three hundred people due to arrive from our depots all around the country – and there was this big snow bomb, a sudden heavy snow storm. It soon became obvious that getting together wasn't going to be so easy.

I was travelling there by car and we got stuck in a traffic jam. The weather was so bad – nothing was going anywhere – that I said to my driver, I think we might need to book a room somewhere to stay over. But he managed to get us to Glasgow – there was no way we were getting any further by car – and I just managed to get the last train heading to Gleneagles.

When I stepped off the train, the snowdrift was up to my waist.

I thought we might have to cancel the whole thing. But to my amazement, when I arrived at Gleneagles and spoke to the person who was running the event for us, he said, everyone'll be here, Matthew, except for two people, but they'll be here in the morning.

I remember the hotel manager saying that if it had been anyone else – any other business – they'd have just have cancelled. It would have been all over. They'd have given up.

It was a proud moment. It was proof that the culture I'd attempted to encourage had been established. Solutions, not problems.

That was probably the best corporate training exercise in Howdens' history – and it wasn't even a corporate training exercise.

Training Days

I'll be absolutely honest, I have always taken a very dim view of the so-called training and team-building exercises that companies drag their poor staff along to, having been dragged along to them myself in the past. A very dim view indeed.

You know what it's like. A typical corporate team-building exercise involves you having to take precious time away from your work and your family and being made to do silly things like raft building or paintballing. I always think that if you really wanted to go raft building or paintballing you could probably organise it yourself and do it at the weekend. If you really want to go paintballing, fine. Good luck to you.

I believe that the best possible training you can give your staff is to teach them how to behave normally, in a civilised fashion, among themselves and with whoever they meet, whatever the circumstances. And you don't do that by sending a depot manager off to some soulless conference room to sit there all day and listen to some consultant up the front banging on about workplace culture, or spending an afternoon running around shouting and shooting paint at someone wearing a mask and camouflage gear. Would you learn anything from doing that? No, of course you wouldn't. You'd come away as ignorant as when you started, and more than likely bored, resentful – and possibly sore. It's a total waste of time.

I came to the conclusion that the best thing to do when it came to training and setting targets and strategy – and all of that corporate sort of thing – would be to take our people away and put them in an environment where they could relax and talk to each other naturally and normally, without too much interference, so that they could establish networks and relationships and be able to work things out for themselves. I wanted to get them away from the pressures of everyday life, to be able to think more clearly about the business.

Which is how we ended up holding our away days at the Coniston Hotel in Skipton. These were entirely separate from the Gleneagles trips, which were a reward. The Coniston Hotel was fundamentally about business.

We first visited in 1998. My idea was simple: you give people time to relax, to get to know their colleagues a bit better, and have a bit of fun, and guess what? That allows them to work together more naturally and harmoniously, to sort out any problems, and to get things done.

Shared experiences in new and different places are extremely powerful and important. I always knew that it was important that our away days should be held somewhere in the countryside, far away from distractions. If you get together with your colleagues in a town or city there are always going to be a few people who'll go off the pub together and then the group becomes fractured and you get little cliques forming and you've ended up doing more harm than good. At the Coniston Hotel we've been able to get people together and get them to stay together for long enough to get to know each other and to really be able to think about the business.

A couple of days at the Coniston Hotel, then off to the Bella Napoli restaurant in Cross Hills near Keighley in the evening, where they used to have guy called Cosimo who would sit in the corner and play the organ; there might be fifty or sixty people in there, and we'd be singing and dancing. It used to get so riotous they had to keep all the windows shut, so as not to disturb the neighbours – and then we'd all troop back to the buses and back to the hotel. A couple of days of that, getting to know people, talking things through, and everyone would return to work fully refreshed, and with new ideas and plans.

That's a training course. *That*'s an away day.

Barcelona Balloons

We also used to have what I liked to think of as our up-up-and-away! days – hot air ballooning.

If you're running a business, you not only need to know your team, you need to trust your team. And what better way to get to trust your team than being confined together for a day in a wicker basket a thousand feet above the ground? It's exciting, it's challenging – but it's also stress-free. You're not actually piloting the balloon. But you have to behave. You have to treat each other with kindness and respect. There's no slamming of doors or storming off in a hot air balloon. It's a treat – but it also teaches you some important lessons about being together.

I'd always liked the idea of hot air ballooning, and one day I was at the Angel Inn and I met a man named David McCutcheon, who happened to be a hot air balloon pilot. I said, David, could you get eight people up in a hot air balloon together? And he said yes, Matthew, no problem. You just need a big basket.

Culture.

A culture based on shared values, working relationships built, in part, by sharing unique experiences.

Ballooning in Spain...

...Dinner on-board The Royal Yacht...

...Reward events at Gleneagles

The only trouble with hot air ballooning in the UK is the weather. So David would take our teams away once a year to Barcelona to go hot air ballooning. If you've never been, I'd recommend it: the excitement, the calm, the bird's eye view, the camaraderie.

The Royal Yacht
and *One Man and His Dog*

Going to Gleneagles, going to the Coniston Hotel, the hot air ballooning – these activities are all about putting time aside to get together, to get to know each other, to get things right, in order to be able to get things done.

I remember in 1997 watching the Royal Yacht *Britannia* leaving Hong Kong for the last time – it was pouring with rain. I watched it on TV. It was quite a spectacle. Chris Patten, the last Governor of Hong Kong, and Prince Charles, sailing away.

Then by chance, many many years later, we had a dinner on the Royal Yacht *Britannia*, where it's now moored, in Edinburgh. And I ended up talking to the commodore who was in charge in 1997, who told me that he was summoned to the Admiralty in London before that final mission and was gently reminded that he'd had a very successful career, but that if for some reason anything went wrong with the departure from Hong Kong, it would be the only thing that anyone remembered him for. So, he was told, the important thing was to get it right. Do not rush, get it right. If you need more time, take more time. The Royal Marine band will keep on playing. Whatever it takes, get it right.

People sometimes say that, in business, timing is everything – you've got to rush through things, you've got to come up with the instant answer. You've got to get in first. It's rubbish. The most important thing is to get the desired result.

It's like *One Man and His Dog*, the old BBC TV programme about sheepdog trials, where you'd watch people competing to herd sheep into their pens. You'd get some young fella trying to rush things and all the sheep would be bobbing about all over the place and it was a total mess. And then you'd get some old bloke and he'd just be leaning on his stick and you'd wonder how he was ever going to shed those sheep. But he was just biding his time, because all of a sudden there'd be a moment and his old dog would run through and just like that, the sheep were shedded. And the dog would just sit down, with the old guy still leaning on his stick.

Don't rush. Take your time.

Don't just do it, do it right.

The Rat on the Table
and the Old Machine

Take your time, don't rush. And be prepared.

Mike McIlroy, who was my production director at Magnet, taught me a few lessons about preparedness over the years.

Thinking back, they were lessons I'd already observed from the example of my own family's business. I remember when

I was young, my father brought in some new machine to the tannery and they just got rid of the old machine, sold it or scrapped it, swapped it out, whatever – the old machine was gone. And of course they discovered when they got the new machine up and running that it wasn't nearly as fast as the old machine – because over the years the lads working on the old machine had figured out various tweaks and fixes to get it working far beyond its capacities. And so they wished they hadn't got rid of the old machine.

So – don't always assume the new machine will work any better. Because it won't.

At Magnet, Mike would always put a new machine alongside an old one and keep the old one running. It was only when we knew that the new machine was running properly that we would get rid of the old one.

Also, all machines break down – especially the unbreakable ones. So you need to plan for all eventualities. There is no excuse for not being prepared. If you are running a business, you have to make sure that your business has a future. It's your responsibility to focus on the long term and not just the short term – obviously. It's a truism and a cliché to say so.

But Mike understood this stuff instinctively. If we were at some function or a dinner, it would always be Mike who would turn to me and say, I think we've got all we need to get out of this now, Matthew, it's time to go. Staying any longer is just going to lead to a nasty hangover.

He applied the same idea to the business. Plan ahead. Think beyond the moment.

Here's what that means in practice. For us at Howdens it's meant investing in dual running of our supply lines, securing double capacity. So, our cabinet-making facilities are the best in Europe. But what if we lost one through fire or catastrophe, what would happen? Who would supply us? Surely someone would? But what if they couldn't? Or wouldn't? To be secure as a business, we'd have to invest in production facilities entirely separate to what we've already got – we'd need to invest in spare capacity. Which is exactly what we've done. The same with our IT and computing systems: we have dual systems all set and ready to go.

It's turned out to be a wise move.

No one could have predicted Covid – but because of the lessons taught to me by old-timers like Mike, and then reinforced by long-term thinkers like Rob Fenwick and Will Samuel, we effectively managed to Covid-proof the entire Howdens business. Due to the two-metre social distancing rules, we had to reduce staff on the production line by about a third, which slowed output – so thank goodness we had another production line sitting there ready to bring us up to full speed.

Some people call this cathedral thinking, or just planning beyond the grave. You know the saying, a man of wisdom plants a tree, knowing he will never enjoy the shade. Well, Mike's foresight – and the foresight of many others – has enabled us to enjoy some shade.

Fortunately, Mike and I were always on the same wavelength with this sort of stuff. I always used to say to Mike, it's not about *if* – because bad things *will* happen. It is guaranteed, in business, as in life. It's about *when*. It's about being prepared for when those bad things happen. And of course because I'm me I always liked to illustrate my point with one of my stories, harking back to my days with Old Bill and his hut at JPA in Huddersfield.

Let's say you've got a rat on the table, I'd say. And you've got four bricks and a book – you know the rat is going to come out, and it's only coming out one way. We don't know exactly when it's coming out. We don't know when it's going to make the leap. But it is definitely coming out. So we'd better be prepared.

Bibendum –
And Then All Hell Breaks Loose

Eventually, in September 2005, it all came out.

For MFI, September 2005 was when the old machine broke down.

For MFI, September 2005 was the year of the rat on the table.

At the start of 2005 I was perfectly happy running Howdens. After a decade we were making about £100 million a year, the business was growing, I'd built a good solid team around me. We'd weathered a few ups and downs but we knew what we were doing. Things were looking good. We were set fair.

Meanwhile, MFI had entirely lost its way. It had got itself into a terrible state. They already owed the Royal Bank of Scotland about £150 million. And they were losing approximately £4 million a week. There is no business in the world that can afford to lose £4 million a week. If you're losing £4 million a week you are heading at high speed for the crash barrier. It's only a matter of time.

There had been a massive downturn in UK consumer spending. Sales were down. Rents were up. The share price was down – and falling fast. And the company soon found itself in danger of breaching its banking covenants – which is to say, it wasn't going to be able to meet the terms and conditions of its lending agreement. Which is like not being able to pay your mortgage – or your debts. If you're in danger of breaching your banking covenants you are in serious trouble. There was talk of the whole business being broken up or sold off.

So there was I, perfectly happy running Howdens, which was effectively the trade part of MFI, and one afternoon in late September I get a call from Ian Peacock, who was then chairman of the MFI group. The non-execs had suggested that I should become Chief Executive of MFI – that I should take over the whole business. Would you consider it, Matthew, he asked.

You'd have been mad to have touched it with a bargepole.

There was no easy solution to the problems faced by MFI – any fool could see that. The business was a mess. Plus, if you took on the job of Chief Executive, whatever you did, no one would thank you for it: the banks would hate you, because you owed them money and they'd want you to start selling things to pay them back; the shareholders would hate you because you wouldn't be able to get the share price to recover quickly enough; the staff would hate you, because you'd have to be making some difficult decisions and cutbacks; and finally your own people would hate you, because you'd be leaving them behind to go and sort out somebody else's mess.

So I was seriously considering saying no. Some very clever people had been in charge at MFI. It had been a FTSE 100 business. It had been a mainstay on the high street, and now in retail parks up and down the country. Who's to say I had the answer to MFI's problems? My own branch of the business may have been making £100 million a year, but at the end of the day I was just some bloke from Skipton without a university education who had simply applied some basic principles to running a trade business. And it wasn't as if I was universally liked or admired by the MFI non-execs. For many of them, I was simply the last resort. I couldn't rely on their support.

On the other hand, if I didn't take it on, or if they decided to bring in someone else, then who knew? The banks might have taken over the business, bankrupted the whole thing, betrayed the staff and the shareholders, left the landlords hanging out to dry, and sold off the rest of the business for scrap. Everything would have been completely trashed, including everything I'd worked for with Howdens.

Ian Peacock suggested that we meet at the restaurant Bibendum – a nice place in Chelsea, in the old Michelin building – on Saturday night. It was my birthday, but what could I do?

I started going through the various options. John Hancock, the Chief Executive, had done his best at MFI and had even suggested an MBO – but having been involved with the MBO at Magnet I knew all too well the problems that would involve. As I knew to my cost, an MBO was hugely risky, massively taxing in terms of time and effort, and frankly the banks were entirely unreliable. I also believed we had a fundamental responsibility to the shareholders. With an MBO, your shareholder might have paid, let's say, £1 for their share and you might then buy the business back from them for 20p per share. Which was bad enough. But then you might go on to sell that share for £5 and cash in and cash out. And in my view that's just not right.

In summary, my feelings were that the MFI shareholders didn't deserve to be ripped off, that MFI staff had signed up for the status quo and not for some tricky individual to come in and try and pull off some smart move, and that even if I didn't have all the answers I was at least someone who had the advantage of knowing the business and who happened to be running the only profitable part of it.

So I said yes.

In October 2005 I became the Chief Executive of MFI.

And all hell broke loose.

Just Say No

I was shocked by just how bad things were. Appalled. MFI's costs were spiralling out of control. Sales were in free fall. There were problems with the company pension deficit. There were disastrous and costly IT problems.

I needed to act fast.

I'd met Ian Peacock for dinner on the Saturday. By the Sunday I was ringing round my top team at Howdens – Rob Fenwick, Andy Witts, Keith Sims, stalwarts and stout fellows. I said, If I take this on, are you willing to come with me? And without exception they all said yes, just like that. I remember Rob was cooking his Sunday dinner so it was a very brief conversation. No problem, Matthew. And then he went back to roasting his potatoes. But I knew I had the trust and support of my team. Not a moment too soon.

As soon as my appointment was announced the banks went crazy. I suspected that they wanted to be able to come in and carve up the business on their own terms. For them, it was all over bar the shouting. We had about a £180 million borrowing facility with RBS and we'd already borrowed about £150 million. As soon as my appointment was announced, representatives from RBS were keen to meet me to discuss the terms and conditions of our inevitable demise.

So what was the first thing I did?

I just said no.

I refused to meet them.

I refused to meet them because I knew there was only one way the conversation could go. They would walk away with all the company's assets. I believed that's exactly what they were planning to do. It's not their fault. It's nothing personal. They're bankers. That's what they're programmed to do.

But I wasn't prepared to countenance it – so I just said no. I wouldn't meet the bankers.

As if that weren't bad enough, the business was also at that time about 48 per cent owned by hedge funds, who were happily selling the business short. So it really was a heavy, heavy time – perhaps the most challenging period in my entire career. It called for calm, cool heads – and not just mine.

Cool Heads

For the avoidance of doubt, I am making no claim here to have been the saviour of the hour. But I was certainly the proverbial right person in the right place at the right time, if for one reason and one reason only – I am extremely stubborn. *And* I don't like bullies. I may not be the smartest person in the room, but I won't let other people push around the smartest people in the room. The vultures were circling, ready to pick over the remains of the business, but I just wasn't going to have it. I was going to fight them for it.

Fortunately, I managed to put together a team of advisors and allies who were prepared to join me in the fray – cool heads, super smart, nerves of steel.

One of the major players – a seriously heavy hitter – was David Barclay, a high finance specialist, and who became a key confidante in the battle against those who were seeking to divide and plunder MFI.

There was also Chris Huggins, a merchant banker who worked with David and who was also very wise, the sort of individual who could see the problems with any proposed solution. He was also someone who was very quick to be able to put a value on a deal.

There was Gerrard Hughes, who was the MFI company secretary – and an extremely canny operator. And there was my trusted Howdens team: Chris Youell, Keith Sims and Andy Witts, who were prepped and prepared to keep Howdens in the UK up and running; Rob Fenwick, who had all the skills and knowledge necessary to be able to start working on all matters related to consolidation and MFI's operations in the Far East; and John Watson and Dale Williams, who were in the perfect position to help us look at the business' activities in the US.

There was also Roxy Fry, and Susan Gilchrist, the communications experts, who helped steer me through the seemingly endless minefield of briefings and meetings.

There was Pippa Wicks and Dave Lovett, from AlixPartners, who helped to organise our banking arrangements, and who secured our loan from Burdale, based on a stock valuation. Genius.

There was Ian Peacock, MFI chairman, who helped to manage the whole trauma of the handover before eventually passing the baton on to another trusted ally, Will Samuel.

And finally there was Mark Robson, the one man without whom perhaps none of it would have been possible. In the end, it was Mark who helped us structure the deal that allowed us to take on RBS – and win.

Captain Sensible and the Boring Brigadier

Mark is an extraordinary individual. You'd like him. He is very calm, deep-voiced. He puts you at your ease. He possesses the kind of gravitas that you can't just acquire – I don't know where you get it from. I think you probably have to earn it. Mark is also modest and extremely frugal – the sort of executive who still brings his own sandwiches to work in a Tupperware box. And he has this wicked sense of humour. We laughed a lot, Mark and I, even during our darkest hours.

Before joining MFI in early 2005, Mark had worked in the international metals business. He'd worked all over the world with some – shall we say – interesting characters. One night, for example, about three o'clock in the morning, he received a call to let him know that his boss had been shot by a Russian hooker.

So Mark is unshakeable. And extremely thorough. And he also has the great advantage that he is fundamentally interested in the truth. He doesn't like lies, he won't accept half-truths. And he is prepared to tell it like it is. In the August of 2005, having only arrived at MFI in the March, it was Mark who let everyone know that the business was about to run out of cash. It was Mark who raised the red flag. It doesn't matter what you say or what you hope, he said, this business is in serious trouble. And he could prove it. He knew all the figures better than anyone. Someone might ask some obscure question about what the margin on some SKU is – and Mark will know it off the top of his head. He not only seeks the far distant horizons of truth and meaning, he can describe problems up close and in the finest detail.

In September 2005 it was Mark who famously remarked that this crisis was going to be a job for Captain Sensible and the Boring Brigadier – though who was who he didn't say.

Mark knew that things were going to be difficult. Matthew, he said, I don't know exactly how we're going to solve this, but I do know that it's going to be neither quick nor pleasant.

As always, he was absolutely correct.

Holding the Door Shut

So, I had bought us some time by refusing to meet with RBS, and I had rallied the troops.

And then I shut the door.

This seems to me to be one of the most important and underrated aspects of the role of CEO. It's something that people don't talk about nearly enough. Can you hold the door shut while people get on with sorting out a problem? Can you see off all the predators, the bears and the wolves, the enemies, the time-wasters, the false friends, the endless distractions and petty issues and annoyances that will attempt to overcome you and undermine you? Do you have the strength and the courage to stand your ground so that others can stand theirs?

David Barclay's excellent advice was, Matthew, just don't panic, buy some time, so you can do the right thing. Don't let them rush you into anything.

So I acted fast to slow things down. My message to the banks and to the hedge funds and to everyone else who was eyeing us up was that we needed time, and that I wasn't going to let them in until we'd had time to think. If you want to come and make trouble, fine, but you're going to have to get past me first.

As a leader, when faced with a serious problem, you have to be able to stand your ground. And you have to be able to identify those who might be helpful in coming up with a solution – and those who might be unhelpful. Some you have to bring in, some you have to keep out. There are often people on your own team, within your own ranks, who are really your enemies: hostile shareholders, hostile non-executives, hostile bankers. As a leader, you need to make sure that those who are most likely to cause trouble don't get an opportunity to do so. There will also be people within your own team who will really be genuinely struggling to cope with the problem. They'll become disorientated, or they'll start to panic. They may misunderstand what you're trying to do, or they'll want to urgently implement their own solutions, perhaps something that's worked before. They have to be treated with respect, but you have to keep them out also, so that you can focus on the problem. The people you need on board, you need to get on board. And the rest, you need to keep out.

One evening during this period, Mark Robson and I were huddled around Cazenove's boardroom – the old investment bank and corporate advisors – doing our best to come up with a plan. It was dark outside, late autumn. We had piles of paper everywhere. It was getting late and some banker or other wandered in and asked if we wanted the lights on. The answer was no. We didn't want the lights on. We just needed to be left alone. We just needed time to think. We *literally* needed the door shut, to be left in peace, in the dark, to try and work out the problem.

And we did. No one should have been able to get out of that mess. But we did. We found a way.

Hold the door shut – for as long as you possibly can. Get the right people working on the problem. And then you might have a chance.

Insider Outsiders

I am not part of the Establishment, but I have always admired what I think of as Establishment mavericks – those people who are part of the Establishment, but not really a part of the Establishment. The counter-intuitive thinkers. The insider outsiders. David Barclay was one of those people.

I first came across David when he was an advisor to MFI. He eventually became a very good friend.

He was a brilliant man, David. Phenomenally bright, articulate – a man completely in charge of his own abilities. He was one of those rare people – someone who actually knows what they're talking about.

David's advice during this period was crucial. Slow down, hold the door shut – but then when it eventually came time to act, once we'd worked out the plan, he was ready. He was a doer, a fixer. Leave it to me, he said, once we'd made up our minds what we were going to do – and so we did. And David was as good as his word.

If you ever say, leave it to me, like David, you'd better mean it. You'd better be able to deliver.

Leaders Don't Have All the Answers

To be honest, I don't really have a lot of time for advisors or gurus, or businessmen and women who set themselves up as uniquely gifted or insightful, as the only people with the right answer to this or that problem. I don't trust them. I don't believe them.

Nor do I have a lot of time for so-called turnaround specialists or break-up specialists, or consolidation specialists, or consultants or academics who come up with grand theories about business and who suggest that if you do this or do that, or adopt this method, you'll solve all your problems.

I am not interested in those sorts of people at all. I think they're ridiculous, actually.

David was an exception – an advisor who really knew how to advise, and who knew how to act.

And then there was Ron Heifetz, founder of the Centre for Public Leadership at the John F. Kennedy School of Government at Harvard University. Ron was entirely unlike David, but he also made a big impression on me. David helped guide me through this difficult period, as a person and as a friend; Ron's ideas have helped guide me in my thinking about the business now for years.

When John Hancock first took over at MFI he rightly identified that there were some problems and he brought in some consultants to try and sort out those problems. One of the people he brought in was a man named Gerry Joiner – he lived in San Francisco, Gerry. He was an impressive sort of chap. He'd done some work with NASA after the Apollo 13 disaster. An interesting man. He really had only one message, which was, what is your business really about? What are its values? And how do you as individuals measure up to those values? He didn't have any answers to those questions, of course, and John eventually asked Gerry if there was anyone else who could give us a little more insight, to help to take us to the next step, who might be able to help. Well, said Gerry, there is one person. But he's very difficult to get to see. He's a Harvard professor. If you want to see him, you're going to have to take the board to Boston.

So off we went to Boston to see Professor Ron Heifetz. He spoke to us for no more than about an hour. I liked him. Because he was absolutely clear. He suggested that as leaders we needed to admit that we didn't have all the answers.

So if you haven't got all the answers, what are you as a leader supposed to do?

According to Ron, you have to be able to let people talk. Particularly when there are problems – and in business there are *always* problems – you have to let people talk about the problems. You have to be prepared to relieve the pressure that builds up when people don't talk about problems. You have to help them name the problem. And then you have to let people work at the problem until they find the solution. And you have to give the work to people to implement their solution, rather than trying to do it all yourself.

I liked Ron a lot. Many years later, after all the MFI problems, I got in touch with him and asked if he might be able to come over to the UK and talk to us. He said he was too busy. He couldn't afford the time. But I really wanted him to come. He'd been a great inspiration to me, and his ideas had helped me to clarify my own thinking during the MFI crisis. So I explained to him what our business was all about – it's about kitchens. And kitchens are really the centre of our homes, and of our lives. A kitchen is about families and friends – it's where all the big decisions get made and where everything happens. And Ron very kindly said he'd come and talk. In the end, he came over to Gleneagles a few times. He was always very intense. And his message was always the same. In business you have to let people work things out for themselves.

Different people call this different things. Some people call it decentralised command. You can call it whatever you like. All I know is that it works.

Here's a simple example – a silly example.

I remember once we were at the Coniston Hotel. We were having one of our Howdens away days – some sort of event for depot managers – and we'd organised to have a vintage car run. So we had all these beautiful old cars lined up – and the plan was we were going to drive up to the Lake District and then back again. And so we were all standing there, ready to go. And the person organising the event said, Matthew, who's going in what car? And I said, I don't know, we've got some cars, we've got some people, what's the problem? Well, he said, we have to tell everyone which car they're going in, and which route to take, and what time they've got to arrive, and etc, etc. And I said, I'll tell you what we'll do, let's not do that. Let's tell everyone to divide themselves up among the cars, we'll meet up around one o'clock for lunch at such and such a place, and we'll see them there. And as if by magic, people divided themselves up, got in the cars, drove off, we all met for lunch, and then we all came back.

It's a bit like Bomber Command during the Second World War, trying to sort out the aircrew. I remember hearing this story when I was at school – they knew they had so many captains, and so many navigators, and so many back gunners and so on, but the problem was how to organise them and allocate them into crews. So what they did was put them in a hangar, give them all a glass of beer and told them to sort it out among themselves. Which they did. Humans will find a solution. If you interfere too much it's not going to work. Let them sort it out.

I've seen it happen time and again: the best thing you can do is to enable people to work things out and make decisions.

When we were first selecting the depots for Howdens, for example – they were all different sizes, with different requirements for this and that and the other. How will people know where all the racking should go, I was asked. I'll tell you what, I said. We'll get the manager to sort it out with his staff. I'm not going to tell people where to put their racking. They can decide for themselves. People are not stupid. And you can't legislate for every eventuality.

Now, the MFI crisis in 2005 was clearly on another scale entirely from us working out where to put the racking in a depot in Orpington. But the same principles applied.

You have to admit you don't have all the answers. You mustn't pretend that you have all the answers. But there *are* answers. And there are lots of very capable people out there who are willing to help you find the answers. All you have to do is work with them, hold the door shut to be able to work at it and work it out. And once you've worked it out? You have to act. You have to decide to actually do it.

And you have to convince other people that you are actually going to do it.

No Plan B

Most people thought there was no way we could survive. Massive debts. Falling sales. Pension problems. People were lining up to tell us there was no hope. And the share price kept dropping. Shareholders started losing so much they wanted to come and see me personally. Standard Life owned about 20 per cent of the business – they were particularly worried about the falling share price. I couldn't say no to Standard Life. I agreed to see them. We set up a meeting.

There was me, two of our advisors, Pippa Wickes and Dave Lovett, who were with AlixPartners, one of the big consultancy firms, and the Standard Life man. So we're talking about the business and I explained what our plans were and the Standard Life man says to me, right, but you have a plan B, yes? And I said no, this is it. And he said, are you sure? And I said, absolutely. This is all we've got. There is no Plan B. And off he went. And Pippa Wickes and Dave Lovett were saying to me, do you have any idea who that was? I had absolutely no idea who it was. It was someone called David Cumming. It turns out he was the highest profile fund manager at Standard Life: he *was* Standard Life. I didn't care who he was. I was telling him the truth. There was no Plan B. It turns out that later he said to our chairman, if I could have bought more shares there and then I would have done.

Mr Cumming realised that we had a plan and that we were going to carry it out, come what may – because there was no Plan B.

Rough Diamond

The plan, put simply, was this: we were going to have to split the business. We were going to have to divide MFI from Howdens, allow the Howdens model to flourish, and somehow start to face up to the various MFI legacy issues, one by one.

It may have seemed like a problem that was impossible to sort, a Gordian knot, but in the end, the solution was simple. What it required was an Alexandrian sword – to cut through the whole thing.

I called the solution Rough Diamond.

In Antwerp or wherever, when they're looking at a diamond in the rough, it can take a long time to decide how to cut it. A diamond cutter is going to be looking at a diamond and trying to work out what the best way to cut the diamond is in order to ensure maximum return on investment. With MFI and Howdens I knew there was value in the business, and that the value was derived from, owned by and owed to our investors, the pensioners and employees rather than to the banks, but I knew that to realise the value was going to take a lot of work.

I remember very clearly setting out the proposal, hand-written, on half a page of A4, titled simply 'Recommendation':

There are two very different businesses with different customers and declining synergies. One needs accelerating and one needs a new business model. To have a chance to flourish they need to be apart. The issue we face is that our resources are not limitless – we can't do both at once. Our priority is to deliver value for our shareholders and we believe that this is best done by focusing on the well proven Howdens model and the opportunity of geographical expansion, small central overheads and streamlined supply.

Gerard Hughes, who was MFI company secretary, agreed that we could probably split things up – in theory. We could do it relatively easily on paper, but in reality it was going to be much more difficult. In fact, it was massively complex. There were lots of different ways of doing it. We could close this. We could invest in that. We could separate this from that, or that from this. We could shrink things here, we could grow things there.

Everyone had their own ideas and opinions. But in the end, what you can't have when you're cutting a diamond is lots and lots of options. In the end, you have to have a simple choice: you're either going to cut it this way or you're going to cut it that way. You have to spend a lot of time looking at all the different options. You have to delegate people to investigate the various possibilities – but eventually you get it down to a choice between two. You then have to examine them carefully – and choose. And both those options need to be viable. It's often the case in business – and in life – that people present you with two options that are very similar, and so the choice doesn't really matter. Or they come up with two options, one of which is entirely feasible while the other isn't really an option at all, so in fact there is no choice. The best thing to do is to come up with two options that are absolutely workable – and then you have a real choice. It allows you to test both options to the maximum: this or that, either/or.

In the end, we had our choice. We could split the business and keep working with MFI in an attempt to revive its fortunes alongside Howdens – split and keep – or we could split the business and attempt to find a buyer who would be prepared to take MFI off our hands at a negative price, with Howdens responsible for MFI's multiple legacy issues – split and sell.

I remember very well Mark Robson and I presenting this final choice to the board. It was a tense moment. In the end, we chose to split and sell.

In 2006, Merchant Equity Partners bought MFI's retail operation for £1 – in a deal brokered by David Barclay – while retaining Howdens. The company became known as Galiform PLC. Two years later, in 2008, MFI Retail went into administration and Galiform – of which Howdens was a part – became liable for the costs associated with the remaining forty-six MFI stores and their leases, with Howdens effectively facing debts of £99.7 million. So, it was a bold move – and it took a long time to work things through. Mark Robson was absolutely right: the job was neither quick nor pleasant. But that decision to cut the knot – to work out what to do with a rough diamond – was relatively simple.

The Pie of Pain

MFI's problems were absolutely vast. And they went back a long way.

It wasn't just the over-rented properties. It wasn't just the pension deficit. It wasn't just the problems with the computer system. It wasn't just about having too many factories. It was *everything*.

Mark Robson called it the Pie of Pain – however you figured it, wherever you cut into it, there was always another slice of pain waiting there ready for you to enjoy.

As far back as 1998 Derek Hunt, then CEO, had seen the success of Howdens and had asked me to have a look at MFI. Even then I didn't like what I saw. At Howdens we were working on the basis of local P&L and local motivation, but MFI was entirely reliant on central warehousing and supply and delivery and the whole thing was a tangled mess of local warehouses, central warehouses, main warehouses, showrooms, and kitchen showrooms, homeware departments. I just didn't see what I could do – and besides, I was quite happy doing my own thing with Howdens.

But now it was time to deal with the MFI pie of pain, one piece at a time. In business, success often relies on chunking problems down into manageable bites, which is exactly what we did.

So, for example, the pension deficit. This seemed unmanageable. But we worked the problem. We didn't want to let the pensioners down, but maybe we could speak to the pension trustees and see if we could work on some kind of new investment policy? It wouldn't solve all our problems, but it might make a difference.

The MFI landlords? Yes, we owed a lot money on some very expensive showrooms. But we don't have to pay all the landlords all at once, do we? And some people will want cash, while some people will be happy to do deals. So maybe we can just see what we can do? The great Jim McManus – the old MFI property director – was called back in as a consultant and he formulated deals on every single one of MFI's 108 properties. It took years – it took patience. But it had to be done.

What about the factories? Well, do we really need all the factories? Are there ways in which we can consolidate and combine? We have a small factory making cookers, for example

– are we really any good at making cookers? Perhaps we should invest instead in the things we're really good at doing?

Make no mistake, this was not an easy process. We had to come up with multiple answers to multiple questions – and some of those answers were extremely painful. But in the end you have to find a solution. You have to take responsibility. It's exactly the same as when I was an apprentice in the timber yard. Here's a problem, Matthew. What are you going to do about it?

I won't go through every single thing we had to do – it would take almost as long to describe as it took us to do. But I'll give you a couple of detailed examples – a couple of slices of the pie of pain.

Bloody SAPs

SAP are a big German software corporation who manufacture the systems that these days basically run your company. A SAP system forms the foundations of the digital architecture of any big company. Their software allows you to coordinate billing, order fulfilment, production planning – all of the core operations of your business. So, let's say you sell a door in your Keighley depot, the SAP ensures that the invoice turns up at the customer's house, that the order goes to the factory, and that the factory knows which components are required to fulfil the order. There is almost no aspect of your business that is untouched by the SAP – your financial accounting, financial control, sales and distribution, quality management, plant maintenance, human resources – you name it, it does it. Or it should do it. If the SAP gets it wrong, you don't know what you've got, who's paid you, or what's where. If the SAP goes wrong, you're in hell. You've got chaos.

My predecessor at MFI had spent £60 million on a bespoke SAP in order to try and save the business.

There was only one problem.

It didn't work.

It was a pretty expensive mistake.

This bespoke SAP was designed and developed by some slick American outfit. The promise was, this system would do just about everything except wash the dishes. It would solve all MFI's problems. It launched – inauspiciously – on 1 April 2004, April Fools' Day.

The first I knew about the problems was about six weeks later, when I was in a regional meeting with some depot managers and they were complaining that they didn't know what they had where. They were furious. They looked bad, the depots looked bad, customers were angry. Our immediate solution to the problem for Howdens was to put more stock in the depots so that at least the local managers had control of what they had – but MFI had no room for stock in their showrooms and warehouses, so they quickly lost control.

When I took over at MFI, Dave Hallett became our Head of IT. Dave is another quick-thinking, serious individual, a fundamental man. He saw the problem with the SAP and he said we should just scrap this bespoke SAP and put in a standard SAP. They exist – you can buy them off the shelf. And they don't cost £60 million. It may be basic, said Dave, but we can always make a few tweaks and the main thing is, it's just going to work, straight out of the box. It's tried and tested. So that's what we did. We rolled it out and we have never had a glitch with the system.

So, the lesson from dealing with bloody SAPs – take something standard, then make it work.

Killing All Your Ducks

When things don't work, people get angry. It's understandable. We want someone to blame. The trouble is, the people who are blamed then blame the people who are blaming them, or they blame someone else, and the whole thing spins out of control very quickly and you get a whole cycle of recriminations, counter-recriminations, upsets, outbursts and fury until no one knows what they're saying or doing.

I remember when we were having the IT problems with MFI, and I was sitting in that regional depot meeting with our managers – they really were absolutely furious. They wanted to know what I was going to do about it, there and then. They wanted the IT people sacked. The first thing I had to do was calm things down.

I can go and shoot all the ducks, I said, but you'd better make sure you can quack yourself.

Rather than blaming others, the first thing to do was to see what we could do to fix the problem ourselves. If we can't rely on the system, if we've been let down, if no one is taking responsibility, guess what? We'll take responsibility. Hence the doubling and tripling of the stock held in our depots. So we knew what we had, and where it was. Immediate problem solved.

Now let's deal with the other problems…

Closing Down China

One of the other many things to sort with MFI was the supply chain.

Now, I know that globalisation has brought huge benefits: higher standards of living across the globe; the spread of knowledge and of technology and innovation worldwide; collaboration and the sharing of resources; exciting opportunities for living and for work and for travel. I've been the beneficiary of the forces of globalisation. We've all been the beneficiaries.

But there are also downsides. For our business, in the end, the disadvantages – some of the disadvantages – outweighed the benefits.

When I took over at MFI in 2005 one of the first things I did was to close down our Chinese partnership. This was hugely resisted both by the board and by our own staff. They said it would cost too much to shut it down. It would take too long. Matthew, they said, it's not possible.

My predecessor at MFI was very keen on international trade. He was keen to shut factories in the UK and move production to China. In order to do this he set up a partnership with the Chinese. It wasn't an entirely bad idea. The idea was that there'd be a sourcing partnership in China – we'd get cheap products and we'd retain and invest the profits in the Chinese business. So, if we were currently selling something in the UK for £1 but we could now in theory sell it for 50p because of the efficiency savings in the Chinese business we would still sell it for £1 in the UK and invest the other 50p in China. Which is all well and good. Unless you're a British consumer.

There were other problems with this arrangement. In my first few weeks as Chief Executive I was in a meeting with our Chinese partners and I posed them a direct question. The most basic question of all. If – I said – I bought direct from China rather than through this partnership arrangement, would I get the product cheaper? Yes, came the answer. It would be cheaper for you to buy direct from China rather than through our partnership agreement. So I came out of the meeting and told Mark Robson to shut down the partnership agreement, there and then. The partnership was over.

It was just all wrong, investing more and more money in China – in Chinese jobs and Chinese factories, Chinese infrastructure – and making money in China, rather than in the UK.

I have nothing against the Chinese economy flourishing. I have nothing against global trade. People sometimes think that I don't understand business. But I do. I just happen to think that when it comes to manufacturing, it matters where you buy from. You have a decision to make: you make it here or you make it there. Also, it matters for simple, practical reasons.

If you have a long thin supply chain – with the things you need being manufactured a long way away, let's say in China – you're always going to be at risk of not having what you need when you need it. So for some things – kitchen units, for example – you're going to be better off with a short fat supply chain. Because you're always going to want plenty of kitchen units available, close at hand. Some components you might want to source elsewhere – non-essentials, things you can buy in bulk, items that can be swapped out or changed. But your essentials – the stuff that really matters – you're going to want to be able to source locally. You should always make what it makes sense to make and only buy what it makes sense to buy.

Is this naive? Is it too simplistic? Too short term? Well, let's play a little thought experiment and see where the logic of Chinese production gets you in the long term.

Let us assume, for the sake of argument, that our business is selling kitchens in the UK. We want our customers to have the best price possible and we want to be competitive and survive. So we might wonder, can we buy it cheaper in China? And let's say the answer is yes, we can. Fine. But we might also wonder, if we invested more in this country, in our own production facilities – could we in fact do it more cheaply here? Or will China just always be able to do it cheaper and better? Because they're on a global scale, supplying a huge number of people? Well, maybe that is the case. Maybe China will always be cheaper. In which case, let's be practical, if that's all it's really about, why don't we just forget about the UK and position ourselves as a global sourcing operation? We could then buy all our stuff in China, have all our suppliers in China, and we could supply people all around the world. Of course, we'll give our UK businesses and consumers a little bit of an extra saving, but the profit is in the Chinese international business. At which point we're not really about supplying UK customers any more, we're basically just building a business in China and the UK customer is paying for the success of the Chinese business.

Which is fine. I'm not saying this is wrong. But you might want to try and explain it to your next door neighbour in Darlington or your builder down the pub in Thurrock, assuming that you as a business leader do actually live in Darlington or Thurrock.

Remember, the principle is: worthwhile for all concerned. Not just the shareholders or the owners. Everyone.

Anyway, the long and the short of it is, we closed down China.

Selling Hygena

There was one other extraordinary thing that happened when we took over MFI that helped us enormously. Something that couldn't have been foreseen – another great stroke of luck, if you like.

Luck, plus some rather skilled negotiation.

It was the sale of Hygena. Our quick sale of Hygena was a major coup – it gave us a huge and unexpected amount of cash just when we needed it most.

A man named Malcolm Healey had sold Hygena to MFI in 1987. Hygena was a profitable part of the business, but it wasn't *that* profitable – so when it came to our pie of pain and we were considering what we could sell no one thought much about Hygena. We owed around £150 million in the UK, the retail Hygena business at the time was largely based in France and was making about £2.5 million a year – nothing. The sale of Hygena wouldn't make us nearly enough money – no one was interested.

But Nobia were interested – Nobia are a huge European kitchen manufacturer who at that time had already acquired the German company Poggenpohl, and half a dozen others, including Magnet. They were expanding and they were interested in buying Hygena. The purchase of Hygena fitted right into their strategic aims in Europe – and I knew they were keen. They approached us in a roundabout way and when it came to discussing a price I took a chance and decided to give them the impression that we weren't keen to sell.

In the end we sold Hygena for €90 million to Nobia over the course of a weekend. Which immediately got the banks off our backs – and in one bound, we were almost free of a lot of the MFI debt that had accumulated.

It was entirely unexpected, very fortunate – and got a good business into the right hands at the right time, allowing it to flourish. A round peg in a round hole. It really was a coup.

Now, I know that if Nobia had really understood what dire straits we were in, they probably wouldn't have bought Hygena. They might have waited for us to go bankrupt. But they didn't. They had all the information they required, they approached us directly, they had their own aims and purposes, they offered us what they felt was a fair price – and we got enough money from the sale to fight another day.

Luck? Yes, for sure. Worthwhile for all concerned? Yes.

And fortune favours the brave.

The Thing About Numbers

Ralph, Lord Clitheroe is an old friend. A great man, Ralph. Former chairman of the Yorkshire Bank, former Deputy Chief Executive of Rio Tinto, served in the Life Guards. Stout fellow. We used to shoot together. His advice was always very good, Ralph. Pithy. The thing about numbers and dates, Matthew, he would say, is that in the end they all become one. In other words, in business, in negotiations, people get very hung up on specific numbers or dates – but in the end, they all become one, and you often end up with the figure or date that you first thought of. Useful insight. Good advice. In the end, in negotiations, all the numbers become one.

On the other hand, some numbers really do matter: your daily sales; your Z graph; your projections; all of that.

As it happens, I wasn't very good at maths when I was at school. But I always seemed to have a sense of what was about right – I always managed to get there in the end. It just took me a little longer to work things through. (I was talking to a mathematician once, he was marking some papers on the train, and I was sitting next to him and I said, that looks complicated, and we got talking about maths and he said, I can mark some papers where the workings are all wrong but they still get to the right answer.)

I remember when John Hancock was in charge at MFI, it was felt that I wasn't that good with the numbers. But we had some American consultants in once and they were checking our numbers and one of them said, I don't know if Matthew's exactly good with his numbers, but he sure as hell can feel them.

I certainly can feel the numbers. But I also like to work them through. I like to challenge them. I like to take my time to understand them. If you take time to understand them, they're fascinating. They'll give you all the answers: that's the thing about numbers.

In business you need to know which numbers matter. And which ones don't.

Think Like Feynman

Some years ago, John Foulkes gave me a book about the physicist Richard Feynman. I really enjoyed reading about Feynman. He was clearly one of those hugely charismatic, massively irritating, inquisitive types. He wasn't interested in pleasing people. He wanted to get at the truth. He had to have the facts.

After the Space Shuttle *Challenger* and its crew were destroyed in a catastrophic explosion in 1986, NASA appointed a team to investigate the cause of the disaster. Feynman was a part of the team.

To get to the truth of what happened, Feynman talked to the people who put the shuttle together. Crucially, he discovered that some little rubber seals used on the rocket booster joints failed to expand when the temperature was at or below 32°F (0°C). During a televised hearing, Feynman famously demonstrated how the O-rings became less resilient and subject to seal failures at ice-cold temperatures by immersing a sample of the material in a glass of ice water. As Feynman explained, because the O-rings could not expand, gas found the gaps in the joints, which led to the explosion of the booster and then the shuttle. He got to the truth by asking very simple questions, doggedly and persistently, and by applying some basic logic. Also, Feynman believed that if you couldn't explain something simply to people, you couldn't explain it – hence the O-rings in the glass of water.

MFI certainly wasn't NASA – and I'm no Feynman – but I like the story. I like his style.

Shrinks

Now, admittedly, my style is not everyone's style, any more than Feynman was everyone's proverbial cup of tea. If you're determined, if you're interested in fundamentals, if you won't take no for an answer, if you're prepared to take on something like the MFI mess, or the Magnet MBO, you're probably going to be seen as rather... the nice word is probably 'awkward'. The other word is probably 'difficult'.

Sometime in the early 2000s all of the senior executives at MFI were sent to see a shrink, a psychologist. Why? To try and understand how we thought and behaved, that sort of thing. I wasn't very keen. My feeling was that we had better things to do with our time. But I was persuaded – strongly encouraged – that I needed to go. So I agreed. I'd go and see the shrink. And I decided that I would be completely and utterly honest.

The psychologist was Danish, a man named Ingvar Rosen. He came highly recommended. He'd worked for the Danish air force, apparently, Dr Rosen. In the air force, as in any branch of the military, they obviously want people who can follow orders, but they also need people who are prepared to do what has to be done when it has to be done. Basically, you have to be prepared to kill or be killed. You have to have that fundamental mindset. You have to go from being normal to being – let's face it – rather abnormal.

So Dr Rosen came along to interview the senior executive team. People did OK. They gave the answers they thought were required. I didn't bother with that. I just told the truth.

You had to do all these weird little tests. There were questionnaires to answer. And there were these little boxes you had to look into, which showed a sort of slideshow. You had to interpret all these scratchy sort of images. Dr Rosen would ask, Matthew, can you tell me what you can see? And I'd say, Well, Dr Rosen, I see a coffin on a ladder being dragged upstairs – or whatever. And Matthew, how might you make two plus two make five? Well, Dr Rosen, I'm so glad you asked... Etc. It all took a very long time.

And then Dr Rosen went away and wrote his reports. I still have my report. Most people had areas for development, things they had to work on, categories they fell into. My report begins, 'To say that you are unconventional as a manager and entrepreneur is rather an understatement. It was fascinating to get a feeling for how you have found a personal tailor-made solution to inner contradictive instincts. [...] I have never met anyone who has made such a workable solution for your type of contradictions.' I'm not quite sure even to this day what he means by all that – and there then followed in the report what even Dr Rosen calls a lot of 'psychological mumbo jumbo' – but his conclusion was absolutely fascinating. 'I cannot identify any special need for development. You are developed as a personality.'

Which is nice, though I'm not entirely sure Dr Rosen's test was designed with trade people from Yorkshire in mind. People like me tend to tell you what we really think. And when we say we're going to do something, we just do it. And that's it. There's no great mystery to us really. We're actually quite straightforward. I don't think it makes us particularly odd or interesting. But it does mean we can be very useful – difficult and useful – in business.

One Item Missing

So, with my Dr Rosen-approved unconventional approach, and with Mark Robson's enormous skills, and with the insight and assistance of dozens if not hundreds of others, we slowly put into place operation Rough Diamond and started working through the various MFI problems.

If you were to ask me what was fundamentally wrong with MFI as a business – the basic problem, when all was said and done, when everything was taken into account, all the financing problems, the personnel, the supply chains, everything – if you got right down to basics, I'd say it was the old story of OIM.

One Item Missing.

That was the fundamental problem with MFI. One Item Missing. You wouldn't believe it, but it only takes one item missing – and then another one item, and then another, and another, and another, again and again and again – to ruin a business.

In our industry, in the trade kitchen and joinery business, you really have one job and one job only: can you deliver a kitchen and all the various components of an order, everything that's required by the builder or contractor, complete and in its entirety, in one go, with one trip, in one pick-up or delivery, once and once only? Because if you can't, if there is just one item missing, the builder or contractor is not going to be able to complete the job, which means they're going to have to come back to you, and you're going to have to work out what's gone wrong, and you're going to have to redeliver, which means your costs are increasing, and you're wasting

One Item Missing.

Before Howdens 'one item missing' in the kitchen industry was common place. Fixing this was the central task of founding Howdens... and making profit.

your time, and you're wasting their time, and your business is eventually going to fail.

MFI had a serious problem with one item missing. This was to do with the confusion between local warehouses, central warehouses, the role of the showrooms, a lack of proper stock control due to the failed SAP. It meant that a customer could not be guaranteed to get what they'd ordered: it meant a lot of wasted time and money.

It's easy to get these things wrong. A kitchen is actually a very complex product – there are hundreds and thousands of parts involved in a kitchen. It's like a machine. And if all those parts come separately, flat-packed – and remember, MFI was flat-pack, while at Howdens we were making whole rigid cabinets – well, you can imagine the chances of something going missing.

I remember when I was working for Magnet, back in the 1974. I was at the Bingley depot and a guy in Ilkely was working on a kitchen for a customer who had changed their mind about something – as customers are wont to do. It's their prerogative, they're the customer. Anyway, the builder needed something they didn't have on site and I said fine, that's no problem, I'll drop it in to you. This was on the Wednesday. I drove down with what he needed, but then some other part he needed was damaged so I had to redeliver that, and then something else was wrong – and in the end it took me until the Friday to get everything to him that he needed. Time and money.

One Item Missing = Time + Money.

The Storyteller...

... Dry or complex ideas made useful, accessible and simple

Soufflés

Finally, after the sale of Hygena, and sorting out the supply chains, working with the pension trustees, and consolidating the factories, putting a stop to all the problems with one item missing, we were getting things back on track. We were emerging from the chaos of the MFI years.

At Howdens we had by that time our well-established core product – built-to-last, easy-to-install, low-maintenance kitchens – but in business you simply cannot rest on your laurels, and I was keen to push things forward. I decided that a small, reliable competitive range of kitchen goods was the way for us to go.

My only requirement was that our kitchen goods had to be like our kitchens – absolutely bomb-proof. We couldn't have appliances going wrong the moment people started using them. What's the point of selling shoddy goods? So we started talking to some of Europe's top manufacturers and made it clear we were looking for versatile, reliable, easy-to-fit equipment that didn't cost the earth. Because of our economies of scale we were able to do some deals and eventually found a manufacturer who said they could supply us with a top-spec oven for a much lower price than normal. We also needed continuous production – we never want our supplies to run out – so we also agreed emergency manufacturing contingency plans and the deal was struck. The very first Howdens kitchen appliances were ovens – which we named Lamona.

So – so far, so good.

The trouble was, people – even people in the business – were rather sniffy. Our own sales team started referring to our new ovens as 'pie warmers'. We just weren't getting the buy-in we needed, and I quickly realised that if we couldn't get our own people behind these new products then we wouldn't stand a chance out in the big wide world. I had to come up with something that sent a message to people about the quality of our ovens.

Which is where my old friend John Topham came in. John used to run the Angel Inn in Hetton with Denis Watkins. My wife and I had been frequent visitors to the Angel – the original design and logo for Howdens was conceived there – and I'd often shared a bottle of good wine with John and Denis late into the evening, putting the world to rights. Many years later, John had moved on to bigger and better things, but when faced with my oven issue I knew he was the man to call.

So I sent him an oven to play with and within a couple of weeks he got back to me. Matthew, he said, you have absolutely nothing to worry about. There is nothing wrong the oven. It's a good bit of kit. I said I wanted to know what the greatest test of an oven would be – what would prove beyond doubt that this was a top-quality oven? One word: soufflés, said John. A soufflé requires an even heat throughout the oven. If you want to show off what your ovens can do, show people how they cook soufflés.

So we did.

We set up a marquee in the car park at his restaurant and we had sixteen Lamona ovens set up inside. And then we bussed in all our senior managers and sales teams and sat them down to see what happened next.

John ceremoniously fired up the ovens and loaded eight soufflés in each and every one. One hundred and twenty-eight of the things. If the stunt went wrong the Lamona oven would be finished before it had even begun.

LAMONA

Lamona is the name of Howdens' own brand of appliances.
The name comes from the Lamona breed of Chicken.

To dispel any doubts that Lamona appliances performed well, I had a top chef cook 100 soufflés simultaneously using Lamona ovens.

By the time John had got to the end of the line of ovens the first soufflés were ready – and I remember there was this wave of chatter as each oven pinged and then there was silence when out came one, two, three, four, five, six, seven, eight, all of these lovely, light fluffy soufflés, every one perfectly cooked and then served to the guests. Soufflé after soufflé from oven after oven after oven.

That simple demonstration completely changed the fortunes of Lamona. Our people got behind it, the public got behind it. Sales soared. Five or six years later we'd sold our millionth oven. Lamona ovens now come with a three-year guarantee and an industry, leading aftersales service.

If your people are calling your oven a pie-warmer, show them the soufflés.

Don't Let It Break

Also, just don't let it break. That was my unofficial motto for Lamona.

If you're a single mother and your washing machine fails – that's an emergency. When we sell stuff to our customers, the most important thing is that it mustn't break. And if by some chance it does, the last thing any of us want to do is to speak to someone in a call centre on the other side of the world. Not only do our appliances have to be reliable, we have to have local repair people ready to come out and fix them. It has to work. With a local repair service guaranteed.

Sell what your customers need – and you would want.

That's Going to Sting in the Morning

Slowly, gradually – occasionally in leaps and bounds, as with the sale of Hygena and with the development of the Lamona brand of kitchen goods – we were making progress. 2005, 2006, 2007, 2008 – and then the banking crisis hit.

No one was untouched by the 2008 crisis. Everyone was hit hard. The whole of the banking and business world seemed to cave in. For us, it was almost a knockout blow.

Since 2005 we had split and sold MFI – it had cost us a massive £1 billion to do so. We sold it on the basis that we would be responsible for the MFI pension deficit and the various MFI properties, including the showrooms: the deal was that the buyers would pay the rent but if MFI went bust, the rent would come back to us. And in 2008 they went bust.

That meant that approximately £500 million of debt was coming back to us – and everyone knew that approximately £500 million of debt was coming back to us. We still had the MFI pension deficit to deal with, our sales had dropped by about 15 per cent, our margin was off by about 5 per cent. Any well-educated, numerate person could work out that we had a serious problem.

There's an old Foster's advert in which an Aussie bungee jumps off a bridge and there's a crocodile waiting down below to bite him and the voiceover says something like, 'I'm no expert, but I think that's going to sting in the morning.'

There was a sense in the City that we might have survived the initial MFI crisis in 2005 by some smart manoeuvring but that we were never going to be able to outmanoeuvre a global financial meltdown. Our share price, which had been about £1.50, was now the princely sum of 11p. The company was worth about £60 million. The MFI pension deficit was between £300–£700 million. The liabilities for the MFI properties amounted to about £50 million a year. The numbers just didn't add up. It seemed like no human being could possibly get the business out of such a dire situation.

As always, the banks and the advisors started to make their threats.

I'll be honest, it was a challenge even for me. But as always, the answer was simple – though not easy. Skipton Market Rules. If you have debts, you have to find a way to pay off those debts. And there are only a few ways you can do that. I did a quick calculation and realised that if we put up our prices by 4 per cent that would do it: over time, we'd be able to pay off our debts. We'd survive the crisis.

So that's what we did. I got everyone together after our October sale. I can remember the date. It was 4 November 2008. Remember, sales were down and the margin was down. I got everyone together in a cafe in York and I said to our depot managers, right, unfortunately we don't have a choice. The Howdens way is to leave you to set your local pricing and your margins, but on this occasion I'm not giving you a choice. You either put your prices up or you'll have to send your car keys back. This is what we're doing. There's no alternative. There's no argument. I did the Viking speech. Within a week everyone put their prices up. Burn the boats.

The City people couldn't believe it. It was a counter-intuitive move. Put your prices up when everything is collapsing all around you? It was suicide.

It saved our lives. By the end of November I knew we were going to be OK.

The City – the bankers, the analysts, all of those types – believed that the market simply wouldn't take it, that the support from our customers, the builders, the ordinary working men and women of the country, would simply evaporate and they'd go elsewhere. But that's because most bankers have never been to Skipton Market. They're bankers. They don't understand a business like Howdens. *Of course* nobody likes a price rise, least of all the builders who rely on the lowest quotes they can muster in order to get business. But such was the quality of our supply and our after-sales – such was the loyalty to our local depots, the loyalty to our local managers and their teams – that sales continued stronger than ever, despite the price rises.

The 4 per cent increase saved the business.

Sometimes the only way to deal with a monster is to confront it and kill it – for us, that meant facing facts and paying our debts. Otherwise the problem would keep coming back to terrorise us – that's why we raised our prices. And that's why we're still here today.

The cash came in, we were able to pay off our debts, the business recovered and we started to see the rewards not only in terms of the valuation of the company, but in terms of various accolades and awards – a Royal Warrant, Best Company to Work For, Best Turnaround of the Year. Over the next few years, many good things came to us.

I am not a financial wizard. I don't have the answer to every problem. I'm no dragon-slayer. Sometimes people think there's something magic about the way I do things, or that I know things that other people don't, that I'm just lucky or blessed or charmed. I'm not. Matthew, someone once said to me, it's like you can juggle with rats. I can't.

You want to slay a dragon? You want to beat the crocodiles?

Awards and recognition.

BY APPOINTMENT TO
HER MAJESTY THE QUEEN
SUPPLIER OF FITTED KITCHENS
HOWDENS JOINERY
LONDON

Howdens has been recognised for its outstanding reputation for doing things properly.

Here's what you have to do. Be honest, face up to the problem, find simple, practical solutions – and then for goodness' sake stick to your guns.

Built on Trust

The 2008 crisis was an important reminder that our business is built on trust. People have got to trust you. Whether it's your staff, your customers, your suppliers, your shareholders, whoever it may be, people want to feel that they're trusted and that they are trustworthy.

Part of the reason we made it through the 2008 crisis was that some crucial investors trusted us. I remember one day after a meeting at a management fund, one of the fund managers there walked me to the lift. Matthew, he said, if we have £50 million to invest – which he did – in the end it comes down to a judgement about the person. Am I investing with this person, or another? You either trust that person or you don't. Fortunately, in our case, they did.

Trust was also important between me, our chairman Will Samuel, and Mark Robson, our CFO: as the top team, the people making the crucial decisions, we never undermined each other. There was no second-guessing, no silly talk, no nonsense.

Throughout a business, in the workplace, trust is essential. There'll always be a few people who are a problem, people who betray your trust. But they are few and far between.

And of course in the end it all comes down to the trust of your customers and clients. At Howdens what we're doing is selling to local builders – and in my experience, local builders are thoroughly decent, highly skilled individuals whose working lives are entirely built on trust. In order to succeed, a local builder has to work extraordinarily hard – they have to run a highly efficient, honest, straightforward business, under a lot of pressure from customers and clients. If you need a door, you need it now. If something's broken, you need it fixed. If you want your kitchen done, you want your kitchen done. And if they don't do things right, people are going to know about it. Builders live and work among their clients and customers, they meet them at the school gates and down the pub. They need to be trusted – and they need to be able to rely on us, just as we rely on them.

So – build your business on trust.

Death and Resurrection

The 2008 crisis coincided for me with another crisis. My father had retired early, aged fifty, and had moved to the Isle of Man. We had a good relationship. I admired him very much.

November 2008: the very height, the peak of the financial crisis. There were all these problems with Lehman Brothers collapsing, all of the debts for the MFI properties were coming back to us, our share price was falling. Our advisors and non-exec directors were telling me that my business was dying – and then I got a call to tell me that my father was dying.

I had to make a quick decision about what to do. Stay or go. I decided to stay and sort things out with the business: things were changing from minute to minute and hour to hour, rumours were spreading round the City. It was round-the-clock crisis management.

And my father died. I wasn't there. I flew out to the funeral and straight back again the same day. But before he died I spoke to him on the phone – he said that he wanted to be cremated and buried in my grandfather's grave in Morley. I told him I'd make sure it happened. I'd sort it.

It was a period of intense pressure. No one believed that I could fix the problems with the business. People were saying we'd need a rights issue. Merchant bankers were telling me that the business was only worth £60 million, we had another half a billion in debt rolling in, and we might be able to raise only another £15 million. I said we were going to be OK. They didn't believe me. No one believed me.

My father believed me.

We had him cremated and I went to the churchyard in Churwell to find the grave of W. L. Ingle, his grandfather. But it wasn't there. I spoke to someone and they said, it's not here, it's up in Morley main cemetery, up by the motorway, you'll find it there. And sure enough, there it was, in a little corner plot.

Things took some time to arrange. I'm not really the mystical or the spiritual type but this really was a very strange period – and strange things started happening. Things started moving around at home. The month my father died there was a photograph of his old car, his actual car – a Bristol 405 – on the cover of a classic car magazine that I happened to pick up. I'd told my father I'd sort things out. I knew I needed to get him settled with his family.

I had a wreath made out of suede leather to put on the grave – in tribute to the old Ingle family business – and when we finally placed my father's ashes in my grandfather's grave it was like a great weight was lifted from me. Extraordinary. I knew I'd done the right thing. He was back with the family. It was done. He was sorted.

And with the money I inherited from my father I was able to invest in shares in Howdens. For the first time, I was really able to back the business myself. It meant I could secure my own family's future. It was his final gift to me.

The crisis was over.

Rolling Thunder

After the chaos at the end of 2008 I knew there was more to do – we'd survived, but now we had to secure our position. I was determined that henceforth we would relentlessly progress.

I always like to have a useful name for a project. It makes it memorable. It's symbolic. I called our new project Rolling Thunder.

I decided that for a year we were going to focus all our efforts on our kitchen ranges – new ranges, new colours, everything. We were going to drive things so hard that we were going to drive our competitors out. Every two months we'd bring out another range – and another – and another – so that things were just getting better and better. We'd become unstoppable.

It worked. We went from strength to strength. Rolling Thunder was the next phase – and I used all the skills I'd learnt over the years to make sure it was a success. I had built a rack outside my office showing all our cabinet frontals – the bestselling was at the end and the rack went all the way along the wall, so I could see at a glance what was selling and what wasn't. It was a way of signalling to people when they came in that I knew exactly what was happening, that I had my eye on the ball, which meant they had to have their eye on the ball.

Simple psychology, driving forwards – Rolling Thunder.

Temper Your Own Glass

People often get the wrong idea about business. In business, a lot of what you're doing is fundamentally creative. It's not an art form, obviously – we're not talking about music or painting – but it is a creative endeavour. You're constantly trying to find new solutions to old problems – or new solutions to new problems. You're trying to find new ways of doing old things. Or coming up with entirely new ways of doing new things. That's what we were doing with Howdens after 2008. Innovation, invention. New ideas. Relentless improvement. As with any creative endeavour, your answers and solutions can prove to be challenging and controversial. And nowhere is this more true than when you are challenging trade demarcations.

I remember when I was at Magnet, part of my job was buying tempered glass. In the early 1980s people got very excited about tempered glass – everything was getting made with tempered glass. The only trouble with tempered glass is that once you've cut it to size you can't cut it again. With laminated glass you can – you can cut it again and again. But with tempered glass, it's like putting cheddar cheese under the grill – once that cheese is under the grill, there's no going back.

In the 1980s, Pilkington in St Helens were a major supplier of our glass – but their glass was expensive and their tempered glass was even more expensive. You had to buy it through a distributor. Pilkington made the glass, they sold it to a merchant who passed it on to a specialist who cut it and then tempered it, and eventually it was sold to you. That didn't seem right to me.

So I found a company in Canada who made tempered glass – I could buy tempered glass from them and have it imported cheaper than I could get Pilkington to sell us their normal glass. So we started buying our tempered glass from them. Which was a good solution to the problem – until we started making our own tempered glass, which was an even better solution.

I think of these as classic Duxbury answers to business problems: Jack Duxbury did it when he started buying timber directly from the south of France; Philip Duxbury did it when he started selling windows and doors directly through the depots rather than through a distributor. They were prepared to ask, what if we didn't do it like that, but we did it like this?

What if you were to temper your own glass?

Wonderment

Finding a new way forward obviously means it hasn't been done that way before – which means there's no map. There's no manual. A lot of people like a manual – it tells them what to do. But finding a new way forward – in business, and in life – means working without a map or a manual. It requires courage and determination to work in this way. It requires a certain kind of mindset. I call it wonderment.

Wonderment is not the same thing as just wondering. It's not just looking and wondering – it's not observation. Bankers and accountants do observation. Wonderment is about stepping further back and pushing further forwards than others are prepared to go and asking what's really going on here. It's imaginative work. It's intellectual work. To me, wonderment means a kind of restless questioning.

Here's an example of the kind of restless, relentless questioning we had to undertake after 2008. Let's say a depot is doing well. Why? Are they attracting different customers? New customers? More customers? Or are the same customers buying more volume? Or are they buying different products? It's not good enough just to say it's a sunny day and things are going OK. You have to be prepared to ask the questions, again and again and again. Running a business is being prepared to ask these simple big questions – again and again and again. It's always easier to rest with assumptions than to ask questions. Asking questions, stepping back, pushing forwards – wonderment – is hard work.

Now, I recognise that this is partly a temperamental thing. I'm talking about myself here. It's me that's driven – unusually, obsessively driven. But it's often the case that it takes an individual who's unusually driven to actually drive a thing.

And if you're not driven? Fine. Try wonderment.

Just Run That Past Me Again?

Just run that past me again: six of the most important words in business. People used to joke about it. They'd tell me something and I'd always be saying, 'Just run that past me again.'

This is partly about me being a slow learner. I really do need you to run that past me again, in order for me to understand what you're saying. I'm not embarrassed about it – I really want to understand. So just run that past me again.

It's also partly not trusting all those middle management types and consultants who talk the talk but who fail to understand the meaning and consequences of their decisions. You have to slow them down and get *them* to think. Just run that past me again.

And it's also partly because in business I think one of the most important skills is being able to name a problem clearly. You have to be able to see what the real question is, even if you don't have a ready answer. Just run that past me again.

I learnt this from Ron Heifetz. The leader must be able to help people set out the problem clearly. *This* is the issue. *This* is what we're facing. *These* are the facts. Once you can do that – once you can name the problem, once you understand the facts, then you can do something about it.

To be clear: people used to joke about it, but it's no joke. *Just run that past me again* – it has serious consequences. It means you are prepared to listen and you want to get to the bottom of things. And once you get to the bottom of things you are going to have to act. You'll have to make some difficult decisions.

It can be pretty tiring. You go into a boardroom day after day when things are bad, or you're visiting depots up and

down the country, and people will be looking at you and quizzing you, and you'll be quizzing them – *just run that past me again* – and sometimes of course you'll wonder, can I really be bothered with all this? The relentless questioning?

Fortunately for me, the answer was always yes. I think it's partly because I had a sense of duty – I really wanted to understand, I had a sense of responsibility – and also because I was just curious. And also because I was always able to focus. I was able to clear out the clutter and focus on what was at hand. It's not necessarily an attractive trait – it can make you seem... single-minded is a nice way of putting it – but it is an important quality for anyone in a leadership position.

In 2005, the question was, is there a viable business here with MFI and Howdens? How big can it get? And what do we need to get rid of? Is the Howden's business strong enough to deal with the burden? What are the issues exactly? *Just run that past me again.*

In 2008, when I put the prices up, we were in a very different situation, but it was still a matter of getting to the bottom of the problem.

Just run that past me again.

Again.

Competitors Are Lifesavers

In business, you obviously have to set out to win. So in a sense, your competitors are your enemies. That's just the way it is. It's business. But that's not necessarily a good way to think. It doesn't do you a lot of favours. Because the truth is, business is more complex than that. Life is more complex than that. Your competitors are your enemies, but they're also your friends and acquaintances and companions – and occasionally, your lifesavers.

When I found myself without a job, for example, having been fired from Magnet, it was Derek Hunt I wrote to, Derek Hunt of MFI, who were Magnet's fiercest competitor. And Derek welcomed me with open arms. An important lesson.

It's happened in my life again and again: extraordinary turnarounds, unexpected outcomes, strange combinations, peculiar allies and alliances, unintended consequences.

Take the example of Malcolm Healey, who set up Humber Kitchens. When I was at Magnet, Malcolm was a competitor, clear and simple. And Malcolm built this extraordinary factory in Howden – which he eventually sold to MFI for £200 million. Which gave MFI access to the most modern, up-to-date factory in the UK. Which meant that eventually, when I had set up Howdens and we needed it most – via MFI, via Malcolm Healey – we suddenly and unexpectedly had access to a world-class facility. In a sense, in some strange way, Malcolm was one of the founders of Howdens – without his foresight, without him spending all that time and money on getting the factory exactly right at Howden, we wouldn't be here today.

The exact same thing happened with the Runcorn factory. MFI were about to shut it down when I turned up with my idea for Howdens. The Runcorn factory had originally been built by Schreiber, for making their rigid cabinets – and back in the day, the Schreiber cabinet was the best in the business. Which meant that with the Runcorn factory, because of Schreiber, because of MFI, Howdens were in a position to be manufacturing the best cabinets in the business. What goes around, comes around.

Malcolm Healey did me another great favour when, years after Humber Kitchens, he set up Wren Kitchens as a direct competitor to Howdens. The Wren Kitchens business model was the opposite to the Howdens model. Wren didn't hold any stock. Instead, they had this incredibly expensive machinery that could deliver a customer order as quickly as possible. At Howdens, in contrast, we had the items already in stock, ready to go. Malcolm had a completely different way of doing things. He was retail. We were trade.

Malcolm's different way of doing things did us a great favour. I remember in 2008/9, when Malcolm was just getting going with Wren Kitchens and we were gearing up with Rolling Thunder, he came out with this fantastic variety of colours at a price that was very competitive. This pushed us to innovate. I said to Rob Fenwick at Howdens that what we had to do was copy what Malcolm was doing, the same colours, the same price. Rob thought we couldn't match the pricing – Wren were just too good at what they were doing – but I asked him to speak to our Italian suppliers and it turned out that there was someone who could do the same kind of thing, at a lower price, so we could compete with Malcolm and with Wren Kitchens. The challenge became an opportunity.

Competitors keep you in condition.

Competitors are lifesavers.

Are You Well, and Are You Going Bankrupt?

It was certainly the case, after the 2008 crisis, when we were still putting things right with the MFI legacy issues – dealing with the leases, the pension issues – that a lot of shareholders were put off investing in Howdens. But some people saw the potential.

Brian Haggas was one of them. Brian had been a non-executive director at Magnet back in the mid-1980s. When Magnet got a bid of £3 per share from B&Q Brian was one of those people who thought we should take it, as did many others, myself included – but my uncle Tom Duxbury was having none of it, and so we mounted the ill-fated management buyout.

Anyway, in 2009 Brian noticed that I'd somehow managed to survive and that our share price at Howdens was around 20p – an absolute bargain, if you really knew what you were looking for. I remember he rang me up – I was in our Enfield depot at the time – and he said he wanted to come to see me at home. He said he might be interested in buying some shares. I rather feared he might have wanted a seat on the board. He can be pretty outspoken, Brian. He's one of us. He's a fundamental man.

Anyway, I remember Brian came round for tea on a Friday afternoon. He arrived at the house, I went out to greet him and – Brian being Brian – as he was walking up the path he launched straight in. 'I've only two questions for you, lad,' he said. 'Are you well and are you going bankrupt?' I said I was very well, thank you, Brian, and that no, we weren't going bankrupt. Brian promptly bought a lot of shares – and never did have his tea.

Some years later Brian eventually sold his holding, having made quite a return on his investment.

He knew a good thing when he saw it, Brian. And he knew how to get to the point.

Boiling Over

As we grew and consolidated our growth after 2008 I knew it was important not to rush to expansion or to begin to invest in pet projects and sidelines. We had to be careful. I wanted steady growth – Rolling Thunder – I didn't want us to explode and then promptly implode. I've seen it many times – boiling over, that point at which a business overstretches itself, tries to do too much, and it all becomes a bit of a mess.

Boiling over: to be avoided.

There are those businesses that boil over and then there are those that just keep at boiling point, doing exactly what they do perfectly well, again and again and again.

If I had to identify a few businesses that have kept at a steady boiling point without ever boiling over I'd pick the following:

- **Mouseman oak furniture:** established by the great Robert Thompson in Yorkshire back in the 1920s. Mouseman have basically been making the same furniture the same way ever since. A great product,

Arts and Crafts style, not a big market, but there always *is* a market. And it's never boiled over.

- **Bettys Cafe Tea Rooms:** another Yorkshire landmark and legend. The story goes that Frederick Belmont, a Swiss confectioner, arrived in London and jumped on a train at King's Cross without knowing where he was going – and ended up in Bradford. He then set about opening a classic English tea room and did it absolutely perfectly, Swiss-style. Everything in Bettys is just right. It's expanded over the years and is now part of the Taylors of Harrogate tea and coffee company. But again, it hasn't boiled over. Like its tea and cakes, it's just right.

- **Le Gavroche:** the famous restaurant. Another family business that hit the right spot early on and has kept on hitting it ever since – one Michelin star, then two, then three. Not just excellent but utterly consistent – at boiling point, always.

- **AGA:** the cooker. Designed – unbelievably – by the Nobel Prize-winning Swedish physicist Gustaf Dalén, who lost his sight and found himself spending much more time at home with his wife, who was thoroughly fed up with all the hassle of cooking. So Dalén took it upon himself to design an oven that was easy to use, always on – and indestructible. AGAs do now what they've always done.

- **Range Rover:** launched back in 1969 or whenever it was, these have never exactly been the fastest or the flashiest of vehicles, but they still do what they do and no one does it better.

Go Where You're Welcome

With these exemplary businesses in mind, we grew and expanded, slowly and carefully, step by step, one depot at a time. One of the keys to our success was only going where we were wanted – and again, as so often, I was lucky to have benefitted from the wisdom and the hard lessons of those who had gone before.

When the Magnet business was growing in the 1950s and 1960s they needed more space for a depot and factory, but the local council in Bingley where they were based at the time wouldn't let them expand – the council just said no. But Keighley council, which was just five miles down the road, were more than happy to provide the land and the planning permission. And so Magnet moved to Keighley. Which turned out to be a win-win for everyone: Keighley got the jobs, Magnet got its depot. And Bingley missed out.

When I started Howdens in 1995 I was given 10,000 square feet from MFI in the Northampton national distribution centre. I remember walking round and saying to Keith Sims, one day, Keith, we are going to need all of this. Which sounded ridiculous at the time – completely ridiculous, nonsensical in fact. One day all this will be ours? We didn't even have any depots at the time, or any staff. The whole of the Northampton national distribution centre! What was I thinking?

Then in 2005, with the MFI crisis, people thought we should get rid of the NDC entirely. But I was pretty sure that we were going to need every inch – and more – and so we held on to it. And indeed, as the years passed, we did need more. And more. And more. But the lease on that building was running out. The landlords had other plans for the site. We were going to have to find another base.

We started looking around. We started looking around Northampton. And pretty quickly we found the perfect location – just off Junction 15A on the M1. It was absolutely perfect. We could build exactly what we wanted – which was about a million square feet of warehousing space – in exactly the right location. But trying to build a million square feet of anything anywhere is always going to be difficult – wherever you are, whatever you're planning, you're going to be treading on people's toes. And sure enough, things got quite difficult. Planning permission was turned down. Our consultants suggested that we'd be able to sort out the problems and appeal and reapply but all these things take time and start to get more and more complicated: you get turned down, you appeal, the next thing is the local parish council start protesting and you've got the local vicar and his congregation chaining themselves to fences and articles in the local papers and it all gets rather awkward and unpleasant. My feeling was that time was ticking and we just needed to move on.

So we did two things, bearing in mind both the lessons from Magnet's experience with Bingley council and the sage advice of David Barclay with regard to all such crises and difficulties: buy yourself time. We decided to renegotiate with our current landlords – an extension of just a couple of years on our lease would be useful, which we quickly secured – while we set out to find somewhere we'd be welcomed. We needed to find a council who were keen to have us there.

That council turned out to be Raunds, just north-east of Northampton. They had a site that would suit – there was a perfectly good building already there and all we needed was a couple more buildings and then we could exit Northampton in an orderly fashion and install ourselves in our new facility, which not only had the warehouse space but also offices and parking, and which had the great advantage of being somewhere we were actually welcome.

Again, I know it's obvious – don't try to push water uphill, follow the pollen path. It's almost too obvious to mention – but if you follow the rules, the basic principles, they do work. That's why they're basic principles.

Go where you're welcome – because in a life of finite duration, why would you do anything else?

A Letter From Len

The expansion, consolidation, the move to our new national distribution centre: it all solved a lot of problems. And of course created others.

At Howdens I like to think that we've always had pretty good relations with the unions. I remember when I first sat down as CEO of MFI, I was told that we couldn't afford to pay people. And I said, erm, no. Not only can we afford to pay people, we're going to give them a pay rise. Every year I was at MFI there was a pay rise of 3 per cent. My track record – Howdens' track record – of looking after our people I think is pretty good. I strongly believe that the people in your business who work hard should be looked after – in good times and in bad. Of course sometimes you have to make redundancies, you have to let people go, and that's hard, it's awful, but at the end of the day your people are your responsibility. If you're with us, we'll look after you.

Now, back in the early 2000s, the truck drivers at the Runcorn factory were heavily unionised and were making life pretty difficult for the business there: there were regular go-slows at busy times of year and all sorts of sharp practices. The drivers were Liverpudlians – they were tough people. And I speak as a Yorkshireman. I wasn't running MFI, I was running Howdens at the time, but I was convinced that MFI really needed to sort things out with the drivers, because the last thing the business needed was that sort of problem. If you don't sort that sort of problem, it'll come back to haunt you.

In the end, MFI outsourced the work to DHL – the drivers became employed by DHL. And MFI just hoped that the problem would go away. It didn't.

When I took over at MFI I was absolutely determined to clear up all the legacy, residual problems: paying the landlords, dealing with the pension fund, everything.

Rob Fenwick, who was running the factories and the distribution, came to me to talk about the DHL drivers. They worked for DHL, but it was an exclusive contract, so they only really worked for our factory in Runcorn – and we were moving towards a nationwide distribution strategy, based at our new centre near Northampton. Anyway, we informed DHL we were moving towards a more central distribution model and therefore their drivers – about a dozen drivers – would need to be based in Northampton. We offered them jobs elsewhere, but they refused.

The first thing was a letter from Len McCluskey, General Secretary of the union Unite. It's outrageous, wrote Len. We need to sort this out. Give me a call. I did not give him a call. The last thing I was going to do was start negotiating with Len McCluskey on the phone.

The next thing was people turning up to demonstrate at our offices – placards, banners, megaphones, the full works. Then they started demonstrating outside our investors' offices in London. Fair enough.

Then people turned up in the village where I live, asking people for information about my exact whereabouts, leafletting, spreading rumours and lies. It all got quite nasty. The police weren't interested.

We had to get ACAS involved. And in the end – thank goodness – the issue was resolved. It took time. But we got there.

I'll be totally honest, this was all very painful and very difficult, a colossal waste of everyone's time and money, and one of the toughest times during my entire career.

When you get a letter from Len or his like, you know that trouble is coming. Be prepared.

Always Go to Finland

Of course I have regrets. I never really trust people who say they don't have regrets. What, they've never made a mistake? Ever? They've never done anything wrong? Nothing? No bad thing has ever happened to them? Everything is just fine?

I have plenty of regrets.

One of my biggest regrets?

That I never went to Finland on the old *John Bluhm*.

The *John Bluhm* was a cargo ship that used to bring our timber from Scandinavia – this was when Magnet were breaking the agent-merchant importing chain, breaking the old trade structure, rather than having to go through all the middlemen. We used to bring the timber directly into Scarborough, and it would dry out in the mud in the fishing port, and we'd then take it from Scarborough on a daily basis to Keighley. The *John Bluhm* used to take three or four days to cross the North Sea and in the winter, if the Baltic froze up, they couldn't get it moving, it wasn't going anywhere. It might sit there for days, weeks even.

And there were a few opportunities for me to go to Finland and come back on the *John Bluhm* – but somehow there was just never time. I was always too busy. But I wish I had.

If you get a chance to do something odd or interesting or out of the ordinary, always take it. Nothing comes around twice. That's a serious regret – that I'll never now travel back home from Finland on the old *John Bluhm*.

Cue the Elephants

There are plenty of other moments over the years at Howdens that I'd love to relive – high points, peak moments, good times, from the absolutely sublime to the totally and utterly ridiculous. That's what a working life consists of – they're the things you remember – if you're lucky.

There was the time that Mark Hetherington, who was one of our regional managers, was collecting me from Robin Hood Airport and we were in the car, happily motoring along this long empty road, and we were leaving the airport and I saw up ahead a barrier with a police car on the opposite side of the road. We were chatting away and I suddenly realised that Mark hadn't seen the barrier. We were heading straight for it.

I actually ducked inside the car as we scraped our way under the barrier. The police were laughing so hard that no charges were brought and in the end it was only a small repair bill, but the funniest thing of all was Mark saying to me, Matthew, do you think we can keep this quiet? I said, look, Mark, I think it's a bit too late for that.

Lots of high jinks and adventures all over the world, meeting interesting people everywhere – suppliers, customers, clients. You'd be surprised – you can have some great fun with serious German widget-makers.

I remember once we were in Hanover. I think it was Hanover. Weinig – they make these big woodworking machines and systems makers – were launching a new machine. They have this elephant logo, Weinig – and so of course for this big launch they'd hired a big top with a circus, and there were acrobats and flame-throwers and then the pièce de résistance – or whatever's the German equivalent of the pièce de résistance – an elephant pulling this big new machine into the circus ring, led by the Chief Executive, Herr Wilmsen. Bizarre. Spectacular. Hugely enjoyable. Then someone launched the celebratory fireworks. Cue startled elephant. Cue mayhem. We all survived – and laughed all the way back to England.

Bellissimo!

Germans, French, Italians – over the years we've done a lot of business with Italian suppliers in particular. There's just something about the Italians. They're absolutely brilliant.

We are of course more than capable of making perfectly good quality cabinets and doors in the UK – indeed, at Howden in Yorkshire we do make perfectly good quality cabinets and doors – but the Italians are just able to style it and design it a little bit different. They can design and produce at an affordable price, and then go on to redesign it, tweak it, improve it, just making it better and better all the time. It's a remarkable gift. Bellissimo.

There's someone called Walter Bozza, who has this big company in Italy. Mobilclan. They make the most beautiful solid wood kitchen doors – really beautiful ash doors. Brilliant workmanship, Arts and Crafts-type production at scale, hand-finished on a production line and their logo is a knight chess piece, which they have discreetly stamped in the corner of every cabinet and door. Classy. It's just very nice stuff. And 3B, another Italian firm – they do the high-gloss look. Again, just very classy.

It was John Stephenson – the man who was always prepared – who introduced Magnet to 3B and to Mobilclan and to Walter, many years ago. This was the 1980s, and John was at a trade fair in Milan and he met Walter, who at the time was making these solid wood cabinet doors with oak from Yugoslavia. Could you make them in any design? asked John. Of course, said Walter. So John said, could you do something like these English country house frontals? That was the fashion at the time, this very expensive country house look. Of course, said Walter. And John and Walter really transformed the UK kitchen business by being able to produce these doors that looked just like the high-end country house kitchen frontals, but a fraction of the cost. Quality, service, price: all exactly right.

I learnt a lot from Walter. More than anything I learnt to let people do what they're really good at – particularly if they're

Italian, and particularly if it's anything to do with style. Kitchens are all about style, and the Italians are just obsessed with style, in a way that we can never be in the UK, for all sorts of historical and cultural reasons – so for me when it came to any outsourcing it always made sense to go to Italy for design and manufacture. Not least because if there's a problem, you can get on a plane and you're in Milan by lunchtime and back home in time for tea. It might make short-term sense to have your product designed and sourced a long way away, at the cheapest price possible, but it makes no long-term logical sense.

So – let people do what they're good at. And let Italians be Italian.

The Fundamental Questions

Looking back, one way of looking at a career in business is to see it as a series of answers to a set of fundamental questions. What do I do best? What do we do best? What are our Italian suppliers really good at? What do the Germans do best?

If you can see what the fundamental questions are – if you're really prepared to boil things down and reduce things to the very basic choices – then you might have a chance of making some good decisions. If not, you're going to be prey to every passing whim and fancy. Let's do this, Matthew. Or let's do that. This seems like a good idea. We'll get the Germans to design our kitchens, and the Italians to build the machines. And then we'll have everything made in China. That might work. Well, yes it might. But what are the fundamental questions here? What's really at stake? Disengage, pull back, take a bird's eye view.

Always ask, what are the fundamental questions?

So in my case, for example, in 1989, when the management buyout collapsed at Magnet, the fundamental question was, should I stay or should I go? Should I take the money and walk away or should I stay and see if there was some way to revive the old model developed in the 1940s and 1950s by Mad Jack and Philip Duxbury, the pioneering Duxbury half-brothers, who'd had the vision of a company providing manufactured and prepared joinery from local stock to the trade? Stay or go? Go and forget all about the business, or stay and try and do something with it, revive it, reinvent it. As it happens, I chose the latter. It was an answer to a fundamental question.

And then in 1994, despite the trade model having saved the Magnet management buyout, the new owners wanted to recombine the businesses and there was no longer really a place for me, so it was the same question, stay or go? Stay and deal with the consequences, or go and see if my successful model could be transferred and developed elsewhere? As it happens, I was made redundant. But I had already made my decision. It was time for me to go.

And so on, again and again. Fundamental questions.

In 2005, with the MFI crisis. Could I – could Howdens – shoulder the burden? Simple question: yes or no?

In 2008, with the banking crisis, were we going to be strong enough to deal with the recession and the legacy MFI issues and look after everyone involved? Yes or no? Stay or go?

And then of course for me there was the final question, the really big question, that I knew was coming eventually.

Could the Howdens model flourish in a future beyond my leadership?

Yes or no?

The Final Question

Only a few people understood that I even had to ask the question. Not many people. And fewer still who were prepared to ask the question for me. There was *one* person, someone in HR – Gareth Hopkins – who always felt able to say controversial and difficult things. Gareth is great. He's like me – difficult but useful. And one of the most difficult and useful things he ever said, some years ago, was, Matthew, do you think maybe it's time to go?

I'll be honest, if you create something from scratch, out of nothing, something that's yours and that's connected to your family, it's very hard to step away. But in the end, step away you must. The question isn't *if*, it's *when*. You have to ask yourself the fundamental questions – and allow others to ask, too.

For me, I started to wonder about my future around 2014. We'd just about sorted all the old MFI problems, the business was doing well and I remember we had an autumn meeting with our shareholders and I had this end of summer term feeling – as if I was at school. You know that feeling. I felt for the first time that my work was done, that something was complete, that I was satisfied, and that the long summer holidays were ahead.

It was partly a gut instinct. It was partly observation: I've seen enough people who have stayed on past their sell-by date, and others who have got out at exactly the right moment. For me, it was also a matter of principle. The most important thing to remember – and plenty of Chief Executives forget this – is that a business is not just about you. You've got to think about your staff and customers. You've got to think about the evolution of your business, beyond your own contribution. All businesses go through phases: start-up, development, consolidation, validation, challenge, reconfiguration, restart, redevelopment, and so on and so forth in cycles until the end. And as a leader you have to ask yourself whether you're the right person to lead the company through all those various stages. Maybe you are. Maybe not.

I think it's probably even more difficult to leave when you have a successful business that's still growing – because it seems like everything's going OK and you're doing all right, so why on earth would you go? Why mess with the system? Why upset the apple cart?

Why? Because if you're still growing and expanding you're going to need to be bringing new people into the business, with new skills and new ideas. And you have to ask yourself: are you really the person to be bringing them in and bringing them on? In your thirties and forties, yes. In your fifties, fine. But in your sixties, your seventies, your eighties? You're still the person who's able to see the long term and the future? Really?

So anyway, around 2014 I started thinking seriously about my long-term future. I might be willing and able to hang on, but my senior colleagues would eventually be moving on – and then what? I'd put together an entirely new senior management team? I'd work on building those relationships and bonds of trust and understanding, over years and years? And I'd be entirely prepared for them to challenge me, and they'd be prepared for me to challenge them?

If you're the sitting incumbent and you have your team around you and you're doing OK there's a mystique that starts to develop around your decision-making. Which is not good for the business. The old guard doesn't want things to change. And you don't want things to change. You need people who are prepared to press for change, who won't sit back and rest on their laurels. You need people bold enough and eager for the challenge.

And anyway, eventually your trusted lieutenants start to drift away. Our IT guy, the great Dave Hallett, who'd fought to keep our IT systems based in the UK – a significant factor in our success – decided to retire. It was a big blow. Trying to find Dave's successor was difficult. And there was also the prospect of finding a new chairman – our chairman Will Samuel was coming up to retirement and I really didn't fancy working with another chairman. A chairman's job is to hold you to account. And you have to be prepared to be accountable. And I wasn't sure I was.

Leadership isn't just about what you do at the beginning or the middle of an adventure, it's also about what you do at the end. When do you call time? How do you exit? Exactly how do you step aside? And when you leave, have you prepared others to take on the leadership challenge for the next stage of the journey?

If you're any good as a leader, you're always going to be looking ahead – towards the far distant horizon. It's your job. You've got to be able to foresee the end, before it comes and finds you.

So in 2014 I started seriously asking myself the final question: was it time to go?

Facing Facts (Again)

Of course, I considered staying on. But then the question became if I stayed on, for how long – another five years? Ten years? And then retire aged seventy? At which point the chances are you're going to start getting sick. Things are going to happen. Members of your family are going to get sick. Situations are going to occur. I don't particularly like getting old, but I've been around long enough to know that there are certain problems that come with age. It's just a fact. And you always have to face facts.

Also, I had to be honest with myself. For me, getting the business going and setting out to take on all-comers, that's what I really enjoyed. I'll set up my depot next to yours and I'll give it everything I've got and let's see who comes out victorious. I loved all that. I loved building the teams, bringing people on, the whole thing: work hard, play hard, a curry at night and a bottle of Mateus Rosé, a quick debrief and then onwards, together. For me, it didn't get much better than that.

Also, for me, fixing all the MFI problems was massively rewarding: dealing with the suppliers, the unions, the pension funds, putting things right. That was me at my best.

But times had changed, and the business had changed. When I started out, it was an old-fashioned trade business: builders only, lowest price. But once we'd put the prices up after 2008, things became more complicated. Faced with the horror of bankruptcy, I had taken the only reasonable decision: to put up the prices. But the consequence was that the managers were not quite as in control as they had been. They didn't have ultimate control over price. There was a loss of autonomy

– which is what I'd always wanted for our depots, which is what made us special. It was a small change, really – a slight loss of autonomy. But it meant that each sale became just that little bit more challenging and intricate. And then the end-user started getting more involved, the householder – it wasn't just about the builders any more. Mr and Mrs Jones wanted more say in the design and installation of their kitchen. So the builder went from being the principal of the sale to being the agent of the sale – which again was really a small change of emphasis, but it's not quite the same thing. And the business was just bigger. And digital. It was no longer feasible for me to be running everything on my trusty Nokia C2-01.

My role was really with the pioneers, establishing the business and building market share – because if you don't have market share you've got nothing. But of course, after twenty-five years there's less opportunity to gain market share. Your job becomes about improving service, improving efficiency. It's a different phase of the business entirely. I'd seen it through an entire cycle: the idea, the struggle, consolidation, victory. I came to the conclusion that the next cycle needed different people in charge.

So in 2015 I made it clear to our chairman Will Samuel that I thought 2016 might be my final year. I had a meeting that summer, 2015, with Richard Pennycook – who was going to be taking over from Will as chairman – at the Stafford hotel in London. Richard, I said, I don't think I've got many more period 11s left in me.

It took a long time – until 2017 – for them to find the right successor.

But they did.

And I stepped down as CEO of Howdens Joinery Group plc in April 2018.

One Hand on the Brush

Andrew Livingston officially became the new CEO in April 2018, almost four years after I had first started to think about moving on. That's how long it takes. Remember the Royal Yacht *Britannia*: it takes as long as it takes. Don't get it done, get it right.

Andrew was at Screwfix and at B&Q before coming to Howdens. It may have taken us some time to find him, but it was worth it. You need exactly the right person; someone who is capable; someone who has a proven track record; and someone who really wants to do the job. Like me all those years ago, I believe Andrew is the right man in the right place at the right time.

Andrew joined Howdens as CEO designate in January 2018 so we could have a proper handover period, where I took him round the business and introduced him to everyone. It was the smoothest transition between leaders that I've ever been involved in – which is exactly what I wanted.

I'll be the first to admit that his is not an easy job. A new CEO coming into a well-established business is always going to be looking for skeletons in cupboards, little surprises and problems hidden away that they can solve and resolve – easy wins. I didn't make it easy for him – because there were no skeletons in any cupboards. What Andrew saw was exactly what he got – a multinational business, a public company, valued at £2.5 billion. No skeletons, no surprises, no funny business.

I also didn't want Andrew or anyone else to be having to look over their shoulder all the time: I was determined I wasn't

There can only be one hand on the brush.

HOWDENS

Handing over the 'brush' to Andrew.

going to be one of those backseat-driving CEOs, the ghost at the feast, who keeps coming in and causing problems.

So we had the handover period and then came the moment when you actually have to leave. You have to shut the door for the last time.

I remember talking to my old confidante David Barclay and him saying something very wise: when you're the boss you not only have to decide when to leave, but when you leave, you have to decide to actually leave. You can't pretend. You can't hold on. You have to let it go.

There can only be one hand on the brush.

We had a dinner at the Grosvenor House hotel and I said a few words – my final speech. I said I'd experienced a few crises during my career – the three-day week, the Magnet MBO, the problems with MFI, the banking crisis, every ten years or so something horrible and unexpected had happened. What's the old saying? History doesn't repeat itself, but it sure does rhyme. And I wished Andrew well with whatever the next crisis might be. As it turned out, that crisis was Covid-19, which turned up bang on time, and I'm proud to say that Howdens has come through it with flying colours – and it's nothing to do with me.

When I left Howdens the share price was around £4.50. In September 2021 it was £9.70. When I left, the business was valued at £2.5 billion. At the time of writing, it is now valued at over £5 billion – and looks set to join the FTSE 100. Not bad. Not bad at all.

Andrew's done it.

One hand on the brush.

The Environment of Success

For me, Howdens wasn't just a business. For me, Howdens was the embodiment of an idea about how we should live and work together. If there's anything like a legacy, I hope that's what it is – I'd call it an environment of success, a place where people feel they can contribute, where they are listened to, and where they feel they can belong.

I always wanted people to feel valued. I always wanted them to be rewarded for their hard work. I always wanted them to feel respected and to feel like they were a part of something special. I wanted people to be able to know themselves – and to be able to prove to others – that this really is a good place to work, where good things happen, and where you get to have the occasional adventure.

Above all, I always wanted to create a working environment where people can trust each other to get on and do what's necessary for the business.

Creating that environment of success was why I stayed so long and why I worked so hard – and in the end it was what allowed me to leave.

The Top Twenty

These days, now I'm retired, people sometimes ask me for my top business tips. They want the shortcuts. They don't want to hear the whole story. They don't want to know about the endless difficulties, the near-misses, the might-have-beens, the detours, the cul-de-sacs and the dead ends. They want to know how they can get to where they want to get as quickly as possible, and with as little effort.

I can understand that. But the truth is, there are no shortcuts. There is no direct route to success in business. But there are some basic principles, things you should and shouldn't do.

This is not an exhaustive list. And as you'll see, there is absolutely nothing magical or extraordinary about any of the things. It's all pretty much common sense – what's difficult is having the courage to put these things into practice. Very few people can apply any of them consistently – and if you can apply all of them consistently, well, then you are going to have a very successful career indeed.

1. **You are always too busy to be late.** Which means that five minutes early is on time.

2. **Take time to get it right.** And there is no time to get it wrong. Remember the Royal Yacht leaving Hong Kong.

3. **Tell your story.** This requires you to have an actual story to tell. And to be able to tell it.

4. **Fail forwards.** There are only two directions on the towpath. Forwards, or backwards. Learn from your mistakes and move on.

5. **Skipton Market Rules.** ALWAYS apply. They trump everything.

6. **Recruit the right staff and remember that leopards don't change their spots.** Leopards don't change their spots, goes the old saying. It's true. But it only goes so far. When you're running a business, you need to be very careful about the people you recruit, because once they're in, they're in – and if you then decide you don't like their spots, you're going to have to change your leopard. The trouble is, all leopards have spots.

7. **Distinguish between what is central and what is local.** And remember that what's local is what's central.

8. **Keep your costs low.** Lower. Lower. Lower.

9. **It's not the good times that make you.** It's the hard times that ruin you. Invest. Save. And plan ahead.

10. **Reward your staff.** And not just financially.

11. **Wonderment.** Works – but remember, it is work.

Remember... all leopards have spots...

...if you don't like the spots, find another leopard.

12. **Market share = awareness x specification x availability.** The Jeremy Cecil-Wright formula.

13. **Always want to win.** Because if you do, you might. And if you don't, you won't.

14. **Build myths and legends.** Because man does not live by bread alone.

15. **Make it worthwhile for all concerned.** Because if it's not, it's not worthwhile at all.

16. **Don't say you're an investor in people.** Seriously, don't. Just invest in people.

17. **Blame is a heavy industry.** Don't ever get into it.

18. **Do what you say you are going to do.** It just saves you and everyone else so much time and stops you looking like a fish stranded on the sand. Don't look like a fish stranded on the sand.

19. **Never ever trust a bank.** Sorry, bankers. But you know it's true.

20. **It's not about what you can make.** But how much you can afford to lose.

The Business Killers

Along with my top twenty tips and handy hints, allow me from my privileged position of looking back to suggest a few things that are absolutely guaranteed to kill your business.

These are related to the top twenty to-dos – and like that top twenty, this is by no means an exhaustive list. There are plenty of other things that will cause you terrible headaches and upsets, but the following are all absolutely guaranteed to ruin you and your business. Beware.

1. **Being late.** See the Top Twenty, number one. Being late once is excusable. Twice is a problem. Three times, you're unreliable. I have never met anyone who likes to be kept waiting.

2. **Old stock, damaged stock and unbalanced stock.** People sometimes say that your reputation is everything. In

business, your stock is everything. If it's old, damaged and unbalanced, your business will fail.

3. **Bad debt.** Not all debt is bad debt, but bad debt is very bad indeed.

4. **Depreciation on showrooms.** The bigger and swankier the showroom, the harder they fall. I've seen it, to my cost. Once you've got your big swanky showroom you are going to need to heat it, clean it, maintain it, refit it – a big swanky showroom is an absolute money pit.

5. **Local delivery vans and drivers.** If you really have to do local deliveries, hire a local white van man as and when you need him. Done.

6. **Property rentals and property repairs.** An absolute guaranteed business killer: most Howdens depots cost us just £5 per square foot. At MFI we were paying at least £25. As Americans like to say, do the math.

7. **Pointless and expensive advertising.** Local and direct is good. Word of mouth is best.

8. **Employing too many staff.** You have to get the balance exactly right: too few, you're going to have a problem with your service, culture and morale; too many, you are going to lose your business.

9. **Inappropriate opening hours.** You need to be open when your customer needs you to be open, not when it suits you.

10. **Too much overtime.** The Howdens bonus model solves this problem – everyone in a depot gets the same bonus, equally divided among them. Overtime can crush your business.

11. **Managers undermining staff and the business.** Alas, it happens, because humans are humans. And when it happens, it needs to be dealt with swiftly and effectively.

12. **Poor culture, welfare and incentives.** It's not that difficult to get right. Treat people with respect. Fix the leaking roof. Send a proper Christmas hamper. How would you want to be treated if you were working in this business? Because, guess what, you are working in this business, and so is everyone else.

13. **Nit-picking.** Always focus on the big picture, not on the tiny, irrelevant, annoying details that send everyone crazy and waste their time.

14. **Poor service.** Do you want to be served by rude, indifferent, stressed-out staff with no clue about the business? No, you don't.

15. **Unanswered calls and messages.** If you're not getting a reply, something's gone wrong with the business. People at every level need to be authorised to sort things out and respond.

16. **Not telling the truth.** There is an utterly simple and yet often extremely difficult answer to this problem: tell the truth.

17. **Poor forecasting.** Once again I recommend the use of the Z graph.

18. **Poor range of goods.** Your range doesn't need to be extensive, but it needs to be right.

19. **Poor quality of goods.** You might think that this goes without saying. It doesn't. You need to establish your quality thresholds and stick to them.

20. **Failure to establish the lowest cost of production and the lowest cost of supply.** If you don't establish the lowest cost of production and supply, quite simply, your business is going to die. It may not die today, it may not die tomorrow, it may be a long, slow lingering death that takes many years, but I can guarantee without doubt that if you do not ensure the lowest cost of production and the lowest cost of supply the outcome for your business, whatever it may be, is absolutely inevitable: it is going to die.

Again, as always, obvious? Yes?

Yes.

Which again – as always – is why so many people get it so wrong.

These things are almost too obvious to care about.

Which is why you should care about them, before they kill your business.

The Shoot

So, what are you going to do now, Matthew?

That's what people ask me now.

Well, I've always liked the outdoors. I like country sports and country pursuits. I like the people involved in country sports. And I now have more time to enjoy them both – the sports and the people.

I bought my first gun when I was about seventeen. It was from the Otley gun shop. And I went out and taught myself to shoot. At first it was just rough shooting, me with the dog

– and then later, clay pigeon shooting. And then of course one thing leads to another and eventually you start receiving invitations to join a shoot.

I like a shoot. I like the culture of a shoot. But you have to get it right. I like to keep it simple. I like to turn up at 9 a.m., quick cup of coffee, shoot, sandwich lunch, shoot, cup of tea and a bun at four o'clock and home in time for tea. Don't try to get too much out of it.

A lot of what I've learnt over the years about a good shoot comes courtesy of my old friend Frank Boddy. Frank used to work at Magnet. His father ran the family business, an old timber yard in Boroughbridge, and as was common back in the day, just as happened with me, the son would be sent to work for someone else for a while – so Frank got sent to work for my uncle, Philip Duxbury.

Frank is just a few years older than me, but he always used to call me the apprentice. We worked together at the Bingley depot. I remember he always wore a nice smart suit, Frank, and he drove a nice car. He was everything I wanted to be: charming, intelligent, a man who knows how to deal with people. He sold the family business eventually, Frank, and now he runs shoots at Ripley Castle – and he does it exactly right.

Frank's idea of a good shoot is very simple: it should be hosted in a relaxed manner, with like-minded people from all walks of life, no one excluded, with refreshments available throughout the day, including a proper lunch.

To this day, when people say to Frank, how do you know Matthew, Frank, he always says, oh, Matthew? Matthew Ingle? He was my apprentice.

In many ways I was, and still am.

The Happy Rat

My other great love is boats. Even as a child I was fascinated by boats – how to get those little balsa wood boats to go in the direction you wanted them to go in the pond in the park. My father helped me work it out – I remember we made a little catamaran with a couple of sails, one driving the rudder, and then you could get it moving sideways to the wind, no petrol engine or batteries. I remember thinking it was just a wonderful thing, discovering how to make something that could move and steer itself. It was like magic.

It's the same now: rowing, sailing lasers, messing around on the water. I love it. I have this little boat at the moment down in Devon. It's an amazing little thing, a tiny little dayboat, 16 ft, simple, elegant, fitted out by Rustlers down in Falmouth. I had one of their 24 ft dayboats once – tiny again, but too much for me to handle. I remember I was with Andy Witts once down in Falmouth and I said, Andy, I've bought myself a little boat, and he said, well we'd better go and see it. And so we went to the boatyard to see the Rustler 24 and we opened up the shutters and there it was and I remember Andy saying, you're not going to be pottering about in this, Matthew. She's snarling already.

But the 16-footer is just perfect – a little harbour launch, glass fibre, nothing fancy, but fitted out very nicely. You slap a bit of super-yacht finish on her in the winter and she's ready for next season. We've had her for years now and she's still in sprightly condition. The boatyard in Salcombe made me a little pram dinghy, a rowing boat that can fit on top of her – we call it Jess, the rowboat, after Postman Pat's cat. The 16-footer we call the Happy Rat. Which is exactly what I am.

Putting Things Right

Of course, one boat leads to another. And in the spring of 2020 I bought what was left of my grandfather Ingle's old boat – the *Jorvik*, a 17-ton, twin-screw 42 ft canoe-stern cruiser, a once beautiful, sturdy, graceful craft, built by James McGruer of the McGruer yard at Clynder on the Gareloch. More than sixty years old, the *Jorvik* may have seen better days, but I have done my best to restore it and make it good for the next generation.

I mentioned this project recently to my old chairman, Will Samuel, who remarked that this was a bit of a habit of mine. What do you mean? I asked. Doing up old boats?

Taking something and putting it right, he said.

As always, Will had a point.

In many ways my whole career has been about putting things right. One way of thinking about Howdens is to see it as a continuation of Magnet Joinery, the old Duxbury family business. Howdens' success has certainly derived from taking what was good in the past and adapting it to modern circumstances – and what is a joinery and kitchen business if not fundamentally a business devoted to putting things right? Fixing things up, sorting things out. The *Jorvik* is perhaps just another example. But this time it's for me and the family.

My grandfather kept it on the River Ouse at York. It's a properly crafted Scottish gentleman's launch – a beautiful boat. It eventually passed out of the family but occasionally would come on the market and I always thought it would be wonderful to bring it back home. What in fact happened was that when I was retiring and wondering what I might do – get involved in some charity, or get the golf up, the usual sorts of things – I decided to do a bit of research and ring up the last person to sell the *Jorvik*, who happened to be a boat broker. I explained who I was and that I thought the boat had last been sold around 2013 and I was just wondering if he knew what had happened to her, and if the current owners could be traced I might be interested in buying. I wasn't necessarily expecting a response. It was just an exploratory call.

The phone went the following day.

The owners would be very happy to sell, but there were a few repair works to be done... So I went down to see her. She was in Essex, in Chelmsford. She'd been kept on the Humber and had got herself into a pretty sorry state. She had a hole in one side. Rot. Everything slightly broken and tatty. Things were not looking good. I wasn't sure if I could take her on, but the broker said why not ask an expert to come and have a look, and so we called in John Buckley of Harbour Marine Services. John took a look and he thought he could probably do something with her. And to be honest, I felt it was my duty as a family member to do something with her. If anyone was going to put a match to her, and if anyone was going to save her, it was going to be me. So I offered the owners the asking price, and the *Jorvik* returned to the family.

So, she is a timber boat – which seems fitting, given my great love of timber and my years working in the joinery business. I think in many ways the *Jorvik* unites both sides of my family heritage: the Ingles and the Duxburys. Built in 1950, it was commissioned around 1948 and it has a bridge deck on it – it's a cabin cruiser – a strange bridge deck, like nothing else you've ever seen, until you see a photograph of my father on his tank landing craft, the LCT 455. It's almost exactly the same arrangement. I can only imagine that when my grandfather was having the boat made that my father had some sort of input into the design.

The *Jorvik* is a one-off. She's unique. But she's also an important part of history, my history, and a wider history.

And she'll be on the water again this summer.

Keyman

In business there is something called keyman insurance. It's a policy taken out by companies to insure their most valuable employees – the key men and women, the people without whom the business could not function, the people who take the big decisions and who do the big deals.

In order to obtain keyman insurance your key man or woman obviously needs to be in good health, and to be seen to be in good health – otherwise the insurance might be void, and the markets might react.

I remember during the MBO at Magnet, I was sitting in an office one morning and I received a call. There seems to be a problem with your keyman insurance, Matthew.

The problem was I'd never had a doctor. I had no NHS number. I'd gone to school in Switzerland. There were no medical records. To all intents and purposes, there was no Matthew Ingle. The issue eventually resolved itself, of course – a doctor turned up and asked a few questions and the insurance was arranged.

But I remember for a moment thinking how strange and wonderful that was – the keyman did not exist. I did – and I didn't. I was – and I wasn't. I am – or I have been.

There Are No Family Businesses

One of the many hard lessons I learnt from the Magnet MBO was to avoid involvement in family businesses. In business, family loyalties – or indeed disloyalties – tend to compromise your ability to think clearly.

We all know how the story goes with family businesses. The first generation has a great idea – the founders have nothing to lose and everything to gain. These are the glory years – the days of pioneering. With the next generation, they at least have the benefit of having been around to learn how to do things, and they might be able to introduce some new ideas. Consolidation. But by the time you get to the third generation, if the business has been a big success, a lot of the zeal and enthusiasm has gone, a lot of the knowledge has gone, and all the good work done by the founders and the consolidators is in danger of being squandered entirely. That was certainly the Ingle family story, like so many others. Clogs to clogs in three generations.

In any business, the secret of long-term multi-generational success is succession planning – it's about finding the right person to take over at the right time. This is the stuff of great drama because it's the stuff of real life. Power and fame and success – whatever it is – are often the result of a single person's choices and decisions and their ability to pursue those choices in the face of all obstacles and opposition. As time goes by, that energy and determination dissipates and it's down to others to take on the challenge. Are they capable? Are they willing? Is this something they want to do?

I'm sometimes asked to give talks about the secrets of success, how to get on in life and in business, all of that sort of thing, and I think if one is being honest it's very difficult to say because the real considerations are always highly personal, or they should be: what kind of life do *you* want to live; what sort of rewards are *you* looking for; how do *you* want to realise your unique gifts and potential? There's no one way. How could there be?

As far as my own family has been concerned: my son and my daughter have both made their own paths in life, as they should. They haven't followed in my footsteps into the business and I don't think I would want them to.

In the end, family businesses are just businesses, and that's maybe for the best.

Howdens is not a family business, but the story of Howdens is certainly part of a family story. My mother's family, the Duxburys developed the Magnet business, which eventually went wrong, and I was part of the attempt to fix it, which then led to the creation of another business, Howdens, which learnt from the mistakes of the past, both the Duxbury family's mistakes and those of the Ingles, whose tannery business failed after many years of growth and success.

So, difficult stories, complex stories – like every family's story.

The Monster Decisions

But in the end any story can be summarised – and should be summarised.

I fear this book has already failed the Will Samuel Pub Test – can you explain your business to a stranger, what it is and how it's doing, in about thirty seconds, among all the other distractions and hubbub and noise, and before they lose interest and you lose interest and you both move on and start talking about other more important things? Brief, honest, and to the point?

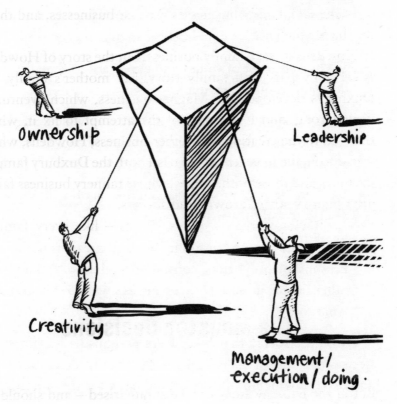

Critical interdependence.

Ownership

Leadership

Creativity

Management /
execution / doing.

If you're anything like me you may have flicked through to the end of this book to see how things worked out. They worked out OK. But you may now want a brief summary, a summing up...

So, in short, why was this business Howdens a success?

I think we succeeded for half a dozen reasons:

1. We had a clear mission and purpose, articulated so that normal people could understand who we are and what we do.

2. We told an engaging story about our prospects that our staff and investors could believe in and engage with.

3. We had clear set of values and expectations that determined our behaviours.

4. We created an environment of success in which people told the truth, listened to each other, and could enjoy and participate in an enterprise that was worthwhile for all.

5. We were prepared to engage and take action, daring always to fail forwards.

6. And to the best of our ability we kept away from the Establishment – banks, consultants, advisors and all those other people in business who always want to tell you what to do.

I would also say that there were perhaps half a dozen big decisions – monster decisions – that really determined our success and which have formed the basis for the story of this book.

These were decisions that were often scary, difficult to handle – and which often seemed counter-intuitive. (The really counter-intuitive decisions were crucial – and never-ending. In 2008/9 alone, for example, the obvious thing for us to do was to reduce prices and margins in order to guarantee sales. We increased prices and margins. The obvious thing was to freeze or reduce pay. We increased pay. The obvious thing was to reduce incentives. We increased incentives. The obvious thing to do was not to spend on property deals. We spent £12 million.)

So, in summary, the truly Monster Decisions:

1. My decision in 1989 to stay at Magnet and do my best to save the business and my own reputation – and to suggest we split the business into trade and retail.

2. My decision in 1994 to approach Derek Hunt at MFI with my idea for a trade business.

3. My decision in 2005 to take on the role of CEO at MFI.

4. My decision to sell Hygena for €90 million, which solved the MFI banking problem.

5. My decision to split the business – Rough Diamond. To separate MFI from Howdens.

6. My decision to raise prices at the height of the global financial crisis in 2008.

7. My decision aged sixty-one to hand over the business to a successor.

That's seven, the big decisions.

But there was probably one more monster decision that really guaranteed the success of the business – marrying my wife. This was way back in the days when you get engaged and then got married at your local church, went to the local hostelry for lunch, and that was it. And for us, that was it – that was the foundation stone for the business. We had absolutely no money, we bought a house we couldn't afford, and I had to find the money to pay for it – which was the best decision we ever made. It pushed us on. As did having children, and moving on, and moving on again. An anchor can also be a propeller.

But if you've flicked to the end of this book and you're really just interested in the scoreboard at the end of play, this is how it looks for Howdens, in simple terms today:

- Over 800 depots

- 4 countries

- 10,000 staff

- Nearly £400 million profits per annum

- A business valued at over £4 billion

Monster decisions, big returns.

Acknowledgements

People sometimes ask me what I miss about the business. Do you know what I really miss? It's a cliché to say it, but of course it's the people I miss.

I miss talking to Keith Sims about his finches. He used to keep finches, Keith. And Keith could *really* talk about his finches. Zebra finches. Gouldian finches. He was a judge at finch shows. He knew exactly what made a good finch, the difference between show birds and breeders. (A breeder has no neck. Show bird sits up well.) I used to love listening to Keith talking about his finches.

And I miss talking to Andy Witts about his sheepdogs and his Kunekune pigs.

That's the joy of our business, getting to know people, being with people. You can never get enough of that. Because one of the great challenges of starting and running a business – that no one really talks about – is that it can be a very lonely task. Getting Howdens established and keeping it going, a lot of time was spent making difficult decisions that required me standing my ground and standing up for what I believed in – day in, day out, for years.

So you need people – good people you can rely on. Not just on a day-to-day basis – your team, your colleagues, your staff, your investors. But also those people – dozens of people – who you get to meet in the ordinary course of life and who teach you and inspire you. At my age, most of those who taught me and inspired me are no longer around. And yet their spirit lives on in the values that they helped to create – and which

I hope are as relevant now as they've ever been. I know I've mentioned many of these people here in these pages, but as a final roll call, allow me to acknowledge the many great and the good, without whom none of this would have been possible:

- 'Mad' Jack Duxbury, who pioneered the way with prepared joinery.

- Douglas Baines Ingle, who taught me what it meant to be a useful citizen.

- Philip Duxbury, who invented the depot system, without which, etc.

- Harry Wright, ex-copper and Mad Jack's wingman, the archetypal trusted lieutenant.

- Derek Hunt, who gave me a chance when I needed it most.

- Denis Watkins, who taught me so much about service quality and value.

- David Ogilvy, whose insights were invaluable.

- John Pyrah, of Jarratt, Pyrah and Armitage, Huddersfield Timber Merchants, a man of high values and principles.

- Tommy Thompson, headmaster at Aysgarth School, who let me look after his dogs.

- Mr Wilkinson, our colourful Latin master, who inspired me to have the courage to stand out.

- Dr David Pick, with whom I shared so many adventures.

- John Carter, for his advice to hang on to the wreckage.

- John Stephenson and Walter Bozza, innovators both.

- John Foulkes, Wim Kok, Louis Sherwood, and Will Samuel (serial offender), who all turned up when no other help was in sight.

- John Topham, who rescued the Lamona oven from being just a pie warmer.

- Jeff Kindleysides, who conceived the look and feel of Howdens.

- Roxy Fry, who translated my thoughts so that others could understand.

- Susan Gilchrist, who taught me to communicate in ways I had never imagined.

- David Barclay, responsible for helping us sell MFI, as well as so much else.

- Jim McManus, who may not have been a founder, but who was certainly one of our many saviours.

- John Hancock and Ian Peacock, who bravely continued to invest in Howdens, despite the many distractions at MFI.

- Chris Huggins, who knows how to write, thank goodness.

- Gerrard Hughes, like the Norse god Loki, who somehow found a way to split MFI.

- Dave Lovett and Pippa Wicks, who found a way to refinance MFI and who kept the wolves from the door.

- Nick Reid, banker extraordinaire, who always made the right phone call at the right time, and who taught me what not to say – and when.

- Richard Pennycook, who found Andrew Livingston.

- Andrew Livingston, Howdens CEO, who has taken the burden from my shoulders.

- Brian Haggas, who bought shares when no one else wanted them.

- Mike McIlroy, Keith Sims, Andy Witts, Chris Youell. Trusted lieutenants.

- Mark Robson, who had no fear of the truth.

- Frank Boddy, who calls me his apprentice to this day.

- Ralph Clitheroe, my own private non-executive director and personal coach.

- Louis Johannot, headmaster at Le Rosey, who taught me to be on time and that one hour before midnight is worth two after.

- Steve Taylor and Dale Williams, who helped to get things going.

- Rob Fenwick, who completely understood manufacturing.

- Dave Hallett, master of his craft.

- My wife, my children, my family.

- And all the others, far too many to name – thank you.